The Works of Peace

The Works of Peace

BY EILEEN EGAN

70029

HV544.5
.E28W

INTRODUCTION BY *Patrick A. O'Boyle, Archbishop of Washington*

AFTERWORD BY *Barbara Ward*

SHEED AND WARD : *New York*

This book is dedicated to everyone who participated in the works of peace and especially to those named below who led and inspired others to perform works of mercy for unseen neighbors:

Margaret Mealey
Ruth Craven Rock

Alicia Goenner McCormick
Margaret M. Zemo

Caroline Palmer (Mrs. J.H.)
Estelle Spurck (Mrs. J. Selby)
Esther Scholter (Mrs. Anthony)
Elizabeth Ann Zepf (Mrs. Arthur L.)
Annamay Scott (Mrs. Ulric)
Josephine Fitzgerald
Maurine Patterson (Mrs. A.G.)
Gertrude Kenny (Mrs. Thomas H.)
Mary Mazzarrelli (Mrs. Anthony)
Mary Lowery (Mrs. Sylvester A.)
Christine Zivko (Mrs. Thomas)

Margaret J. Buckley
Manila C. Caprine
Mary C. Kanane
Anna Baxter
Anna K. Ballard (Mrs. J.V.)

Contents

Introduction

Long before the Peace Corps, the Catholic women of America had their own Peace Corps. I was happy to be present at its birth, when leaders of the National Council of Catholic Women expressed their wish to have their own channel for overseas aid. They pledged wholehearted cooperation with the arm of mercy of the bishops of the United States, Catholic Relief Services—N.C.W.C., of which I was then Director. They offered further aid in special programs that expressed the compassion of woman's nature.

Catholic women had little idea in 1946 that their works of peace would extend so far around the world and so long into the future. The efforts of the Foreign Relief Committee seemed a valid but brief response to the human need that cried to heaven immediately after World War II.

The first recorded women's club in our country, we are told, was founded in Wiscasset, Maine, in the Thanksgiving season of 1805, when Mrs. Silas Lee and thirty of her friends formed the Female Charitable Society. Doubtless, Mrs. Lee would have been amazed to learn that this society was the mother of all the women's clubs which grew up throughout the United States. Through these voluntary associations, the women of a democratic society pooled their talents and resources to meet an infinity of local needs. As time went on, local organizations, particularly those that were church-related, became national federations. When the United States was catapulted into a central role in world politics and world aid after two global wars, the women's organizations transferred to the world scene and to their far neighbors the priceless experience gained in local service to their near neighbors. The National Council of Church Women, the Federation of Temple Sisterhoods, Hadassah, and the National Council of Catholic Women had parallel development in this regard.

The programs of the Foreign Relief Committee have developed alongside the over-all relief effort of the American Catholic community through Catholic Relief Services—N.C.W.C. Women helped to personalize a massive relief effort and to focus on specific needs in a great sea of want. Lifelines of aid extended by the committee have been strengthened every year since 1946, and new methods of cooperation have developed. I will mention only the self-help projects for refugees in Hong Kong and the training courses in homecraft, hygiene and nutrition for the mother and child on four continents. In less than two decades an immeasurable amount of good has been accomplished, and this book tells the story for the first time.

It is a story alive with dramatic encounters and unforgettable vignettes. We see Mother Teresa of Calcutta in her white homespun sari addressing thousands of women assembled in the desert resort of Las Vegas, and we learn of her New York meeting with Mother Dengel—an unexpected encounter of two of the twentieth century's most notable Mother Foundresses. We can follow Mrs. Giny Vachal in her escape across the Iron Curtain, to her eventual contribution to Catholic women's activities in the United States. We are given the story of how Mrs. Mary Hannan Mahoney offered up her sufferings so that in death, as well as in life, she helped her African sisters.

We are brought close to the reality of hunger in the world. The dark drama of family suicide looms before us in the gutted Korean landscape. But we go beyond the anguish, to the fact that those who are merciful not only lift the unhappiness that burdens others, but find happiness for themselves through their works of mercy.

We know that the valiant woman of the Bible "reaches out her hands to the poor and extends her arms to the needy." The valiant women of America have found ways to reach out in help, not only to those around them, but to the needy of the world. Until our time, women played little or no role in the political development of the nations of the world. Still less was their voice heard in international decisions, except for the peace-making efforts of such saints as Elizabeth of Portugal and Catherine of Siena.

It is a rewarding experience to read a book that recounts so vividly how American women brought to the international scene the fruits of their creative and healing gift of compassion.

Take up this little book on the works of mercy and you will see how they are the truest works of peace. Mercy, we all know, is only another name for love. It is love responding to need, love going out to meet the needs of the person loved.

Works of peace are more necessary than ever, for in a nuclear-fragile world the only right relationship between man and man consists in the works of mercy, and it is woman who will remind us of this most crucial fact.

Patrick A. O'Boyle
Archbishop of Washington

1

Works of mercy
under the six-pointed star

IN a time marked by hatred and indiscriminate violence, American Catholic women have given a witness of indiscriminate love, Christian love that brooks no barrier of race or creed, or the categories of enemy and friend. They gave this witness under the sign of the six-pointed star of the Foreign Relief Committee of their federation, the National Council of Catholic Women. From the beginning of the program, I was privileged to serve as the link between Catholic women and the needy in all parts of the world. I was sent to centers of need in post-war Europe, in India, Vietnam, Hong Kong and Korea, and there I was able to serve as a "stand-in" for millions of American women ready and anxious to meet the human need that was described to them.

I was enabled to fulfill this function because I was a member of the staff of Catholic Relief Services-National Catholic Welfare Conference, agency of mercy of the Catholic community of the United States. I was fortunate enough to be stationed at our headquarters in New York City, which

seemed to be the headwaters of a great river of mercy aris-
ing from fresh springs in the U.S. and separating into trib-
utaries which brought relief to the war-ravaged countries of
Europe, to the misery-scourged countries of the Middle East,
Asia, Africa and Latin America.

People have often asked what led me to become involved
in international service. As far as I can see, I was led to it by
the experiences of my early life and by a temperament which
may well have been influenced and even formed by those
experiences.

The greater part of my childhood was spent in the village
of Cwmgwrach, meaning Witch's Vale, in one of the dark wet
valleys of South Wales. It was flanked by two great coal mines
that ate the heart out of the richly green mountains. The
cave-ins caused by the collapse of supporting timbers, by un-
derground flooding and by a host of causes that were investi-
gated after each dreadful death, were part of the ever-present
fear of the villagers. Every family had someone "down the
mine," and a few days out of every year, the whole village
waited breathlessly for trapped men to be brought to the
surface. We all knew the question to ask—"Is there a handkerchief over his face?" This was the mark of death. In the
life I knew, violence haunted man in his work and in his
natural surroundings.

The violence that haunted our everyday lives was intensi-
fied by the history of the British Isles which we studied
throughout grammar school. We were always learning about
men and women who had been beheaded, drawn and quar-
tered, hanged, pressed to death under heavy stones. We were
the only Catholics in the village, and when I repeated the
stories to my parents, I often had to correct the school judg-
ments on people and events. Mary, Queen of Scots, was a

prime example. In school Mary was a traitor; at home a heroine. At home I was reminded that she was a Catholic and very much sinned against. And this happened in many other cases of Catholics who were venerated at home, execrated at school. It developed after a while that I found myself identifying with the person who was hunted and executed—the beginning of a lifelong identification with the victim.

As I studied a wider perspective of history in high school and university, I was struck by a less obvious but more pervasive violence, the economic violence that oppressed large numbers of the human race. At this time, our family was living in New York City, where I became acquainted with the ideas and work of Peter Maurin and Dorothy Day. Through articles and the examples of their lives they reminded us that a chief concern of every Christian should be the performance of the works of mercy—those same corporal works of mercy that Christ went about performing for the people of his time on the roads and in the villages and towns of Palestine.

The works of mercy seemed even more imperative when World War II brought the most massive, the most indiscriminate slaughter of human beings ever known to history. With the new methods of warfare, it seemed obvious that if man were to have a future, he would have to learn to be tender with his kind.

Toward the end of World War II, I wrote some articles on the war refugees, victims not only of hatred and violence, but also of indifference. I was called in to discuss these reports with the administrators of the newly founded agency of the American bishops for aid to refugees and the war-stricken. As a result of these meetings I became part of Catholic Relief Services-N.C.W.C. The director, Monsignor Patrick A. O'Boyle, later to become Archbishop of Washington, D.C., asked me to give talks and confer with those women who expressed a desire to use our agency as the channel through which they could reach out to the needy overseas.

As my experience broadened so that I saw more and more of the world's exiled and needy, I was able to convey to the women something of the shattering impact of being uprooted from one's home and homeland, of facing the world stripped of possessions, of family ties and of any stake in society. In these talks, I had to choose a few individual cases as typical of hundreds of thousands. In picking a single face out of the mass, one could help Americans to confront personally what had been to them the great faceless misery of homeless, starving humanity.

In writing *The Works of Peace,* I have often done the same thing—not only in writing about those who have been helped, but also in describing the women who have been the helpers. Each case must stand for an untold number of others. It goes without saying that a catalogue of the total program of the National Council of Catholic Women, or a catalogue of the many marvelously dedicated women who have made real contributions would have been too long for a single book.

Any book is the vision of one person. This book is my vision of an immensely varied program that reached out to touch the lives of most of the peoples under heaven. This chapter gives a backbone of chronology on which to hang the examples and tales of the later chapters. These, in leaping from country to country, mirror the flexibility of a globe-girdling program for meeting human need. Each chapter stands on its own and develops a certain aspect of the over-all effort.

The first joint activity of the National Council of Catholic

Women in conjunction with Catholic Relief Services was the work of clothing the naked. Those to benefit by this program of mercy were the millions of shorn and innocent lambs—the children facing the first winter of peace in a Europe gutted by war.

To the unknown child

In past wars the chief casualties were among those actually fighting, since battles were conducted on the basis of combatants facing combatants. World War II broke through such rules in favor of a concept of total war. Through the bombing of cities, the use of weapons of mass destruction, and the internment and execution of civilians, non-combatants by the millions were made victims. No one has dared to make an estimate of the numbers of children who fell before the anonymous executioners.

After the First World War, memorials were erected in capitals all over the world to honor the Unknown Soldier—memorials occasioned by the fact that war was becoming more anonymous in its massive power of destroying mankind.

Shortly after World War II the Catholic Church in Central Europe reminded the faithful of the complete anonymity of war when it put up a memorial "To the Unknown Child." This memorial to the children was placed in front of the Church of the Infant Jesus, in Prague, Czechoslovakia. In the stone relief sculpture were the figures of a sorrowing mother and father standing in the ruins of a destroyed city. Lying before them was the body of a dead child. To the right of this scene stood an angel who had gathered up the child for Paradise.

Underneath was the inscription:

Of such is the Kingdom of Heaven.

Hundreds of thousands of innocent children have perished in a war, the most terrible of all the ages. To these little martyrs, the memorial in front of the Church of the Infant Jesus of Prague is dedicated by Catholic Charities in Prague.

Foreign Relief Committee

In 1946, the Foreign Relief Committee was added to the roster of NCCW National Committees. Many months of discussion had served as preparation for its formation. Its immediate aim was to bring help to the children overseas who had survived the holocaust; its larger purpose was to stimulate charitable giving on behalf of war victims and displaced people. It joined the already existing committees of the NCCW, which dealt with such concerns of the Christian life as international relations, home and school associations, and rural life problems.

By the formation of the Foreign Relief Committee the NCCW entered into a cooperative relationship with Catholic Relief Services-National Catholic Welfare Conference, which had been created in 1943 to channel the corporate charity of the American Catholic community to a world in need.

During 1943, Catholic Relief Services could not enter Fortress Europe with any form of aid. Because the war called for a blockade of the continent except for the British Isles and the Iberian Peninsula, the new agency of mercy started with services to refugees in the United Kingdom, Portugal and Spain. Before long, it was bringing aid to groups of scattered refugees outside Europe—in Iran, the Indian sub-continent, the Holy Land, North and East Africa, Mexico.

In 1941, the bishops of the United States began an annual

collection for special needs under the title, "The Catholic Bishops Emergency Fund." This was taken up on Laetare Sunday, the Fourth Sunday of Lent. At first the funding for Catholic Relief Services came from a joint community effort known as the National War Fund. This was discontinued after 1946, and from then on, the Laetare Sunday Collection provided the basis for the aid and rescue programs of Catholic Relief Services-N.C.W.C.

The first groups of refugees were fleeing the persecutions of Hitler, and had somehow managed to steal out of occupied Europe. In 1943, it was already clear that the problem of the refugee would not be eliminated with the overthrow of Nazism. Hundreds of thousands, chiefly from Poland and the Ukraine, were escaping from the Soviet Union by way of Iran. They proved to be a foreshadowing of an unending stream of refugees into Western Europe, South Vietnam, Hong Kong and South Korea.

The American public was due for a long involvement with driven and threatened human beings around the world. Catholic Relief Services-N.C.W.C. brought personnel, supplies and funds to over sixty countries, where its very presence stimulated the formation of local networks of aid to meet local needs. In underdeveloped regions, need meant not only hunger, nakedness, homelessness and untreated illness, but also lack of training, skills and employment for growing populations. From the beginning, help and cooperation were extended by the agency on the basis of need alone, without reference to any other factor.

Catholic relief in Europe

I accompanied the delegation of the NCCW to the first post-war meeting of the World Union of Catholic Women's

Organizations held in Rome in September 1947. The theme was "Woman's Contribution to the World Community," and the meeting was a mirror of the state of the Church. The ancient Catholic lands of Eastern Europe, Poland, Lithuania and Slovakia, were represented by exiles. Shortly before the end of the session, two young women arrived from Hungary. They had been ready to leave in good time but their transit visas through Yugoslavia were held up until the very last minute. They were clearly incredulous at having actually arrived in Rome, and at being able to move about and discuss freely the conditions in their country. There was sparse representation from Germany, but masses of women came from Spain, Portugal, France, Belgium and Holland.

One day, from the podium of the hall of the Angelicum, a slender Polish woman spoke for the Catholics in the Church of Silence. She was Jadwiga de Romer, a Catholic Action leader who made her home in Switzerland. "I speak for millions in Eastern Europe," she said, "when I affirm our unbreakable link with the Holy Father. No propaganda, no separation, no barriers can sever the spiritual ties which bind Poles, and peoples now behind The Wall in Eastern Europe, with the heart of Christendom, the Vatican."

From England came a young woman who gave a cogent address on the challenge to women presented by the post-war world. She gave her talk in fluent French, a language understood by most of the women present. Her audience was large and deeply attentive. Her name was Barbara Ward.

Delegations were there from Pakistan and India, China, Japan and Indonesia. At the meetings in the great *Aula* of the Angelicum, the Rome study center of the Dominican Order, the representatives looked like an ordinary group—an attentive class, say, in the extension department of some urban university. But at the formal audience with Pope Pius XII the Philippine women came wearing dresses like diaphanous butterfly wings, the Spaniards with mantillas flowing from high combs like black clouds, the Indians, with the brightest of saris, looked like long stemmed flowers. The message from His Holiness was the same for all: "The time for action is now!"

After our audience Monsignor Andrew P. Landi, Director of the Catholic Relief Services-N.C.W.C. Mission in Italy, showed us some of the welfare problems of that country with which the Pontifical Relief Agency had to grapple. This was the newly formed Catholic Charities Agency of Italy through which supplies from American Catholics were channeled.

At Rome's outskirts were the teeming new slums, the *borgate,* where ragged children held out their hands for lire, or threw stones at well-dressed strangers who gave no coins. Nearer to the open air cafes of the Via Veneto were the oldest slums in the world, the Roman Baths of Caracalla. Squatters from bombed-out tenements and from the squalid towns of the Abruzzi had boarded up the arches. In the dank stone vaults they made cave-like homes. Their telltale lines of washing gave proof that the ruins were inhabited. On the road to Ostia, the Village of Saint Francis was rising to give new homes to a few of the poorest of the poor.

We saw that the Pontifical Relief Agency had engineered a huge operation to "save the child". From the fetid slum, T.B.-threatened youngsters, sometimes from a family of ten who all lived in one room, were taken to the open country. Most of the food and clothing given the children came from overseas. The volunteers, lay and religious, the organization, the country hospitality, were Italian.

Monsignor Landi organized an excursion for our whole

group to Cassino and the Monastery of Monte Cassino. It was a day of brilliant sunshine, of cemeteries and graves. First on the open plain was the cemetery of the Italian dead, then the well-cared for burying grounds of the French and British military. A small sequestered plot was for the Moors who died fighting with the Allies. Along the roadside were graves marked with German helmets, rough wooden crosses and an occasional swastika. Here were the remains of the German dead.

On the brow of Monte Cassino we stood among the broken stones of the Abbey. Workmen were scurrying about carrying carved angels' heads, bits and pieces of marble and shattered green and turquoise mosaics for careful cataloguing. The tomb of Benedict and Scholastica was almost miraculously intact. The dusky green of the olive trees that had grown on the slopes was replaced by the dead white of naked and scarred trunks. On the opposite hillside was the cemetery of the three thousand Polish soldiers who died defending the already ruined hilltop.

We came down the mountain and stopped at the foot to view a pulverized mass that had once been the town of Cassino. Now it was another cemetery, for the civilians who had been destroyed along with the ancient stones of the town. All we could see was a single jutting wall, a remnant of the cathedral, and a haze of gray dust.

There was no use in trying to rebuild the old town, and the new Cassino was rising nearby. We stopped at the new girls' orphanage which had taken in all the little girls of the area who had lost parents and homes in the battles that had devastated the countryside. In the kitchens were stocks of American canned foods and powdered milk. In the new town square two nuns were superintending a large group of girls who were dancing in circles, now clockwise, now counter-clockwise. All the children were wearing American dresses —bright cottons, a green jumper from some parochial school, a few party dresses with flounces.

"Need I tell you where their clothes come from?" asked Monsignor Landi. "These are your children in need."

On our trip through the Italian countryside, we came upon Genzano. Ruth Craven, Executive Secretary of NCCW, remembered in a special way the name of this town and suggested that we call on the parish priest. Here in the ancient church we saw an image of great interest to American Catholic women, the painting of Our Lady of Good Counsel. The priest turned on the lamps that gave the image a soft glow— here was the representation of the patron of the National Council of Catholic Women.

After the meeting in Rome we went to see the needs of post-war France. In Paris, the office of Catholic Relief Services was inside the large enclosure of the Motherhouse of the Daughters of St. Vincent de Paul. John B. McCluskey, N.C.W.C. delegate in France, put us in the hands of Sister Clothilde Regereau, coordinator of eight hundred social welfare institutions of the order in France.

Sister Regereau in turn took us to meet Mother Decq who had been Mother General of the Order during the years of war and occupation. Before meeting her, Sister told us how Mother Decq had suffered in Ravensbruck, the concentration camp for women.

"Why was Mother General put in a concentration camp?" somebody asked Sister.

"For my crimes! For the crimes of Sister Ann. For any of a thousand crimes. We were all law-breakers in those days. It was a crime to snatch a Jewish child from certain death. It was a crime to help his parents. It was a crime to give shelter to a prisoner of war who escaped—a Frenchman, an English-man, or American. We have houses all over France, you know. Orphanages, hospitals, schools for the poor. The hunted people came to us. They gave us their children. I took three myself. I gave them new names, and found a place in a school. They are alive today with their parents. Our houses in Alsace were filled with men in hiding. How could we turn away prisoners who escaped?"

The Daughters of Charity and Secours Catholique were the channels for American supplies in France. One institu-tion receiving this aid stood out—a shelter for mentally re-tarded boys conducted by the Brothers of St. John of God. We drove out of Paris to visit the home, set in rolling wheat fields. There were three hundred boys, their mental capaci-ties ranging from almost no learning power to the mentality of a ten year old.

Monsignor Jean Rodhain, Director of Secours Catholique, told me that even these children had been in danger of ex-termination during the years of the occupation. I met the director of the shelter and he introduced me to the boys, some of them tall healthy young men, with the untroubled trusting eyes of six year olds. He explained to me how they had saved the boys from the Germans, who could not under-stand why anyone would defend the youngsters. " 'They are useless eaters,' they told us. 'They can neither work nor pro-duce. France would be better off without them.' The offi-cers finally backed down. But they told us that we would have to move out of the main buildings. We would have to provision their men as well as our boys. Our team of brothers had to work twice as hard to grow vegetables and grain, and get produce from the farm. But of our charges, we did not lose one."

I looked at the boys carrying out various tasks in peace and order. What more marvelous vindication could one find of the divine in man than this defense of the weakest, the most deprived of God's creatures.

The President, Board Members and Executive Committee of the NCCW who saw relief work at firsthand in Italy and France were strong and creative supporters of the developing programs of the Foreign Relief Committee. Let us trace the first beginnings of the Children-in-Need program as a case in point.

Children in Need

Once Catholic Relief Services-N.C.W.C. had set up its headquarters in New York City, its next step was to secure warehouse space for the clothing, medicines and material relief of all kinds, which we were seeking. That warehouse was crucial to the operation of the first project of the Foreign Relief Committee, the Children-in-Need Campaign for children's garments.

It might be said that this campaign was sparked by the Catholic women of Lancaster, Pennsylvania, part of the Diocese of Harrisburg. After a talk that I had given to the Lancaster Council of Catholic Women, one of the first to come forward was Mrs. John Devlin, who asked, "What can we as women do for people overseas? Tell us how we can help, and we will follow through."

I explained that on the basis of reports to our headquarters, one of the greatest needs was for clothing, especially children's garments. Led by Mrs. Devlin and others, the women of Lancaster bought up available material, including remnants, and made every conceivable type of children's garments, under and outer, babies' and school children's. These were the first gifts in what came to be called the "Children-in-Need" clothing collection.

After meetings with Mrs. George D. Rock, Executive Secretary of NCCW, and the other officers, it was decided to invite all the affiliates throughout the country to join the work of clothing the naked.

Mrs. Rock, at that time Miss Ruth Craven, held meetings at the Headquarters of the NCCW in the National Catholic Welfare Council Building in Washington, D.C. In discussions, at which I represented Catholic Relief Services, we decided to print a leaflet outlining the needs, and informing American women what garments were needed and where they could be sent. At the same time, the Board officially voted to add to the list of National Council Committees a committee of cooperation with Catholic Relief Services. Mrs. Caroline Palmer, a former National President, was appointed its first National Chairman.

The leaflet, "Children-in-Need," carried pictures of children in the wake of war, and went out in 1945 with the regular bulletin of the NCCW, "The Monthly Message." Relief Chairmen were chosen to function in dioceses, deaneries (groups of parishes), and individual parishes. Children's garments began to pour into the warehouse. The quality of the clothing was extraordinary. A high percentage was new, very often homemade. Garments that children had outgrown were mended so that they were immediately wearable. Missing buttons had been replaced on coats, dresses, shirts and trousers.

The first foreign relief program of the NCCW was thus inaugurated with a stream of gifts. In less than a year, over six hundred thousand pounds of clothes reached the warehouse; the number of individual garments was at least triple that. The clothing was dispatched to Europe and Asia, to be given out to orphans, the displaced and the neediest of needy children.

The corporal work of mercy of clothing the naked became a part of the over-all program of the NCCW. Its members had already been fulfilling this command locally; now through the Foreign Relief Committee, with volunteer chairmen throughout the nation, they were extending it beyond the borders of the United States through the charity network of Catholic Relief Services. All garments were donated by individual women or by women's groups throughout the country.

For newborn babies, thousands of simple layettes were provided. In areas where babies were actually being bundled in newspapers, these layettes prevented illness and saved lives. To those in Europe's DP Camps, the arrival of wearable clothing was like a visit from someone who cared for them, who wanted to make up in acts of charity for the terrible experiences they had endured.

Storehouse of merit

The warehouse of Catholic Relief Services was subsequently moved from New York City to an industrial area in New York's suburbs. It was a cavernous shed with a rough cement floor, longer than a city block. But every Thanksgiving this building was filled to overflowing with gifts of clothing. Donations at this significant season became so much a part of American Catholic life that families began putting clothes aside throughout the year in readiness for the yearly parish collection. "Give Thanks by Giving" was a watchword in homes and parishes across the land. At the height of the campaign three hundred people worked full-time at sorting, pressing, strapping and baling the donations. An assembly line process had to be installed so that the storage space would not become glutted.

Technology was placed at the service of charity in baling machines which pressed the clothing to one-third normal size —an important item in regard to shipping charges. Once compressed, the clothing was held by steel straps, wrapped in waterproof paper and enveloped in burlap from a long tube of sacking suspended from the ceiling. Then from stencils, the addresses of destinations around the world were printed on the packages. Such initial codes as MOC, WOC, COC, Men's Outer Clothing, Women's Outer Clothing, Children's Outer Clothing, soon became recognized in the ports of the world.

The Thanksgiving clothing collection, begun in 1946, reached a peak ten years later, when gifts of clothes totaled close to eighteen million pounds. Collection remained a year-round activity and the warehouse was operated throughout the year for the packing of purchased items and gifts from the NCCW.

A visitor put the huge shed-like building and its contents into a spiritual context: "What a storehouse of merit this place is. Every gift here is an act of charity for someone totally unknown. The only bond is Christ. We are in the presence of a spiritual reality in these mountains of garments."

John the Evangelist asked how we could love God whom we have not seen if we do not love our neighbor whom we can see. The Catholic women by loving an unseen neighbor were proving their love for the unseen God. In time, I was able to report on some whom I had seen wearing their gifts—a

refugee arriving in West Berlin presented with a tweed over-
coat, a woman beggar in Hong Kong wearing a neat cotton
dress, a child playing on a beach in Vietnam in a cowboy
sweat shirt, an old woman selling combs in Korea bundled
against the bone-chilling winds in layers of woolen sweaters
and a stole.

On May 24, 1948, His Holiness Pope Pius XII signed a
special apostolic blessing to every Catholic woman who participated in the collection of clothing for children in need.
Calling the little ones a "Legion of Holy Innocents," the
Holy Father wrote:

> In token of Mother Church's gratitude to the Catholic women
> of the United States, for their continued solicitude for the welfare
> of Her Legion of Holy Innocents, and in pledge of further potent
> aid from on High for their newly consecrated effort to the same
> holy purpose, we gladly impart to you, to each and every member
> of your faithful service group, to their officials, and to all who
> assist them, The Apostolic Benediction.

Papal Storerooms of Charity

The second program of the Foreign Relief Committee of
the NCCW involved a direct line of aid from the Holy Father and the New York warehouse.

Because of the all-absorbing duties of the papacy, Vatican
charity had been placed, as far back as the thirteenth century,
in the hands of an Almoner. It was he who gave out clothing,
food and money to the poor at the gates. Under Pope Pius
XII, the Papal Storerooms were placed under the direction of
a Religious Sister. A new element was added when the
women of the new world engaged themselves in a corporate
work for the Vatican charity.

Under the energetic direction of Mother Pascalina, the housekeeper to Pope Pius XII and Directress of the Papal Storerooms, gifts from His Holiness had reached beyond the confines of the Diocese of Rome, beyond the borders even of the Italian peninsula. Women in Berlin, in Yugoslavia, in remote hamlets of Austria, who had been failed by every other resource of charity, wrote, in their despair, to the Father of Christendom. They asked for prayers, and they often asked for clothes to cover their children. Mother Pascalina, whenever possible, answered these requests with individual packages of clothing, matching as far as possible the exact requests. Such packages must have carried with them a powerful message of the importance of the personal, the individual charity, after the great impersonality of the war years.

In 1946, Dr. Alba Zizzamia paid a visit to the Papal Storerooms. In an article, she described the joyous efficiency with which Mother Pascalina and her corps of Sisters opened gifts to the Storerooms and made packages in response to heart-stopping appeals by mothers, by families, by priests and by bishops.

In 1947, Monsignor Landi took us to meet Mother Pascalina in Vatican City. The energetic Sister brought us to one of the smaller courtyards on the left side of St. Peter's, then through the four rooms that comprised the Papal Storerooms. Donated and purchased garments had been sorted out carefully on shelves. She showed us some of the letters of appeal that came in, and she had a few packages made up to show us how the cards carrying the blessing of His Holiness were inserted in them. Unfortunately, the pleas from Italy and overseas far exceeded the resources of the Papal Storerooms.

In a leaflet I wrote on my return, I presented the needs of

the Papal Storerooms to the leaders of the NCCW. It was decided to hold a special collection to replenish the supplies. Each American Catholic woman was asked to give at least one brand-new article for children, the project's goal being a million garments.

In May 1948, the appeal went out through the NCCW committee system. On the cover of the pamphlet was a photograph of His Holiness Pope Pius XII. His expression was anguished, since the picture had been taken as he addressed a Caritas group on the needs of battered Europe.

The text described some of the institutions maintained for European children, and concluded with a plea to the Catholic women of the United States. "The time is now. It may be difficult to meet and sew during the summer months, but it does not mean a tremendous sacrifice for each and every Catholic woman of the United States to buy or make at least one new garment for one of today's suffering children. It may be possible to buy a whole layette, or a whole outfit, or a new pair of strong shoes. It must not be forgotten that millions of children trudge through winter's snow and ice, with their poor little feet wrapped only in canvas. There is hardly a mother, or a warmhearted woman anywhere who would not want to be the means of allowing the Father of Christendom to present a new and shiny pair of shoes to some litte orphan whose life knows so few joys. Little ones are helped if they are in a need; there is no barrier of race, or politics, or creed.

"Put into the hands of the Father of Christendom the layette that will go to cover the baby, born like another Christ-Child, in a cave in a rock, or a stable, or hole in the earth."

After the first million garments had been received, the women showed no inclination to curtail this charity. Beautiful layettes streamed into the warehouse from every part of the country. There, they were repacked in heavy wooden cases, marked with MAP (for *Magazzine del Papa,* Italian for Holy Father's Storerooms), numbered in a series, and then shipped to Rome. In this way the Father of Christendom was continually able to respond to the desperate appeals that came to him from far and near on behalf of children in need.

When Pope John XXIII came to the Vatican it was thought that he might decide to discontinue the Papal Storerooms. After a visit to the rooms stocked with new layettes and garments for children, Pope John decided to continue this most appealing charity. Mother Pascalina had by that time left the Vatican to give her services to the North American College, and three nuns, of the Congregation of the Franciscan Missionaries of Mary, were called in to staff the Storerooms.

On a visit to Rome with Mother Teresa of Calcutta in 1960, I saw how the big wooden cases packed in the New York warehouse arrived, were unpacked and the garments placed on shelves that reached from ceiling to floor. Coats and dresses were placed on hangers as in a clothing store. Even the heavy packing cases were utilized. The newer rows of shelves had been constructed from the sturdy wood by the *San Pietrini,* the skilled workers of the Vatican. "These are the 'American shelves,' " said Sister Maria Ariberta. "Those heavy ones were made from the Philadelphia boxes. . . ."

It was decided, following that visit, to reorganize the operation of this collection and to rename it the Holy Father's Collection for Children. With NCCW leaders, we worked out a plan to ship one half of the new garments contributed to the Holy Father to destinations other than Rome. Though they would be shipped by Catholic Relief Services-N.C.W.C., they would be given out in the name of His Holiness. Thus was developed the program by which garments were sent in the name of the Pope to help children who were victims of disaster and earthquake in Chile, of homelessness in Colombia, of wretched poverty in Paraguay.

There was general rejoicing at the remarkable quality of the clothing and continued reports showed the women how dramatically the geographical limits of their charity were extended when their donations joined the shipping programs of Catholic Relief Services-N.C.W.C. Homeless and ill children in Calcutta benefited regularly from gifts that came to them from the hands of His Holiness. The children of North Vietnamese refugees felt even closer to the Pope, their "Sweet Christ on earth," when they learned by experience that he was mindful of their needs. New garments, especially First Communion outfits, from the collection for the Papal Storerooms began to play a role in Latin America. This was most fitting, since the Church in the United States had been given a special task on behalf of the hemisphere to the south.

Pope Paul VI gave his blessing to the continuation of the Holy Father's Collection for Children, and his inspection of the NCCW donations in the Storerooms was photographed for the American Catholic press.

All year long our warehouse in New York City received the dresses and suits for First Communion, the layettes, the snow-suits, the shoes, dresses, shirts and pants that made it possible not only to replenish the Holy Father's Storerooms, but also to spread the charity of the Vicar of Christendom around the earth.

One very meaningful letter of thanks stands for many. It came from the region where the Founder of Christendom performed his works of mercy, from the Holy Family Home in Bethlehem, Jordan.

Wrote the Sister of Charity in charge of the home: "I come to thank you on behalf of the dear little brothers and sisters of the Divine Infant Jesus of Bethlehem for the very needed and useful articles of clothing you have had the charity to send them. May His infinite love meet you in the same way, as nothing we do for Him goes unrewarded. We shall ask the God Who was made man here in this very town to pour His special graces on you."

The five-pointed star

Once the works of mercy for the needy overseas were started, they continued to grow in strength. The "Children-in-Need Drive" went on side by side with the collection of new garments for the charities of the Holy Father. The receipt of new and used garments at the warehouse mirrored the special drives and activities in the diocesan councils around the country. Some gatherings yielded a bumper crop of new garments, especially meetings at which the Holy Father's Storerooms were featured. Every year, for example, after the convention of the Winona Diocesan Council of Catholic Women, a carload of as many as twenty thousand new garments was sent to New York for distribution in the name of His Holiness.

In time, new needs developed and were presented to the Board of the National Council of Catholic Women for its consideration on the basis of the over-all reports of the bishops' agencies and in light of the data gathered by the representatives of Catholic Relief Services in the given area. In connection with the acceptance and promotion of new programs, there was first a conference with the NCCW Executive Director, Miss Margaret Mealey, the other officers of the NCCW, the Foreign Relief Chairman, a volunteer, and the Foreign Relief Secretary.

Mrs. Alicia Goenner McCormick, as the first Foreign Relief Secretary, laid the groundwork of the Foreign Relief program at NCCW national headquarters. Pamphlets entitled "The Works of Peace" were prepared at regular intervals. On the cover was always a classic design of a dove by Pico della Mirandola, as a symbol of the Holy Spirit and of the peace that men may achieve by cooperating with his promptings and graces. Through factual data and firsthand accounts supplied to the women in succeeding issues of "The Works of Peace," the story of overseas needs was disseminated to the affiliates of NCCW. Auxiliary material was provided a few times a year through the Foreign Relief Committee page of the "Monthly Message." A short feature called "Foreign Relief Highlights" presented anecdotes relating to the overseas aid effort.

Key figures in the effectiveness of the national appeal were the Foreign Relief Chairmen, those volunteer officers willing to give talks to gatherings of women on needs abroad and on the ways to meet these needs. Mrs. Caroline Palmer of Cordele, Georgia, Mrs. Estelle Spurck of Los Angeles, California, Mrs. Esther Scholter of Milwaukee, Wisconsin, Mrs. Elizabeth Zepf of Toledo, Ohio, Mrs. Annamay Scott of St. Paul, Minnesota, Miss Josephine Fitzgerald of Rochester, New York, and Mrs. Maurine Patterson of Austin, Minnesota, were all effective pleaders for the poor people of the world. They gave talks gratis, and travelled great distances to carry the message of the works of mercy. Each woman brought her own special gifts of mind and heart to her work as chairman of the Foreign Relief Committee. It was fascinat-

ing to see how one would evoke special response for Children-in-Need, a second for Feed-A-Family, another for the
Papal Storerooms and another for Madonna Plan. Each one
mobilized the energies, first of her own community, and
then of the larger Catholic community.

An indispensable factor in dramatizing overseas need to
American women was the presence at their biennial national
conventions of women welfare leaders from the world's most
anguished areas. As many as ten thousand women gathered at
these conventions to discuss the challenges to Christians living in a world of upheaval, rapid social change, and mass
want.

Bishop Edward E. Swanstrom, as Director of Catholic Relief Services, facilitated the appearance of Sister Regereau of
France at an NCCW National Convention shortly after
World War II. Over a decade later he made it possible for
Mother Teresa, foundress of the Missionaries of Charity in
India, to talk at the Las Vegas convention on the need for
works of mercy in Asia; and two years later, in 1962, through
the person of Sister Dulce, he helped present the terrible
dilemmas that confronted the Church in Latin America.

It was Sister Regereau who first gave American Catholic
women a direct report on the impact of their "works of
peace" in landscapes torn by war, occupation, upheaval,
homelessness. She stood before a general meeting of the
convention held in New Orleans in 1948. It was a little more
than a year after we had visited her in France.

While she spoke, the women in the audience followed her
every word on mimeographed copies of her speech. The title
of her talk was "What American Aid Has Meant to France."
She spoke directly to her female audience: "You saw our
misery and—like Veronica—you dried our tears, brought us

comfort—dressed our wounds and gave us the COURAGE to rebuild a new FRANCE. . . . You have sacrificed time, money and energy and you have sent food, clothing, medical supplies and a thousand other items to your needy brothers and sisters across the sea. Yes, dear friends, you have not only preserved the body—but you have helped our Church to give new life to the very soul of France."

In a few words she reminded her listeners of the effects of the war. "The Church of France was dealt shattering blows in the last most destructive of wars—200 institutions of charity conducted by the Church were totally destroyed, while 500 institutions were partially destroyed. Three hundred Catholic schools, built over the generations with so much sacrifice, were completely wiped out, and 500 others were seriously damaged. The House of God would seem to be a particularly vulnerable target in war, since 800 of the churches of France were left in ruins at the end of the war, and 2,000 others were badly damaged by air attack or ground fighting."

Through such vivid presentations of the story of the wounded Church and of wounded brothers and sisters overseas, the foreign relief program gained support throughout the United States. The number of programs grew to five.

The Feed-A-Family program, inaugurated in 1947, brought help, chiefly food, to some of the poorest families in the world. This program, which broadened to become a Help-A-Family effort, is discussed in several chapters, including Chapter Eight.

Operation Hong Kong, described in the next chapter, was directed to the needs of the million refugees in Hong Kong and Macao. This was begun in 1948.

The Madonna Plan was started in 1958 in response to

many appeals, especially from newly emerging countries. Specific details of the program are given in "Madonna Plan Spans the World," as well as in other sections of this book. The Madonna Plan involved Catholic women in a new dimension of overseas aid, that of training. It involved them in a closer partnership with women around the world.

Instructing those in need of knowledge was of prime importance at a time when nations in Asia and Africa were becoming independent, and the cold war had multiplied misunderstanding and vilification. While the end result of the cold war was to separate the human family into opposing camps, the aim of the Madonna Plan was to draw together the people of different races and nations under one Mother.

For a few years the Foreign Relief effort was stabilized at five programs, and was promoted through "The Works of Peace" under the sign of the five-pointed star. The sixth point of the star came with a campaign which seemed to bring the Foreign Relief program to a full circle. Having started with one aim of sending gifts to the unknown child victim of war and disaster, the women were now ready to add to their general overseas relief programs a more individualized form of help.

To the known child

Fifteen years after the start of the Children-In-Need program, another way to help children overseas was worked out as a cooperative effort of Catholic Relief Services-N.C.W.C. and the National Council of Catholic Women. While the aim was the same—to come to the aid of the most helpless members of the human family—there was a distinct difference. Children-In-Need consisted of gifts poured into a great anonymous stream of charity—the garments went to unknown children. The new program called "Help-A-Child" began in 1961. It was individualized in that a specific child received help, and the person giving assistance entered into a personal relationship with him, receiving his photograph, regular letters, and news of his progress every month.

The personalized program was only possible because of the dedication of many persons. Chief among them was Mrs. Margaret Zemo, Foreign Relief Secretary at NCCW's national office. It could only continue because the directors of orphanages in Korea had the sponsored children write detailed letters four times a year and because the Korean office of Catholic Relief Services took on the enormous task of handling the individualized donations for hundreds of orphans every month.

Thousands of children orphaned by the war had to be gathered into shelters to prevent them from dying by the roadside. Priests, brothers, religious sisters and lay people took in the innocent victims of war. Military companies, before leaving Korea, collected funds and left as a memorial a new or enlarged orphanage or hospital. The children had a roof over their heads, a bed to sleep in and blankets to cover them. But the soldiers, through whose generosity the new shelters had come into being, were far away. The thousands of children had to be fed every day of the year. New clothes had to be purchased, and, since there are no free schools in Korea, an orphanage director had to find between two and four dollars a month for each child attending the local school.

When Miss Sighle Kennedy, the Catholic Relief Services-N.C.W.C. Project Supervisor for Korea, returned from a tour of duty that took her all over that country, she told us of the continuing plight of the Catholic child care institutions.

"Those who direct these orphanages are doing their very utmost," she said. "They are burdened with large institutions that grew overnight. There are no resources anywhere in sight in Korea to tide them over these difficult days. A lifeline must be thrown to them from the outside. . . . Undernourished children develop T.B., or they catch it from sick children that are left at the orphanage door. Korean families, seeing their children sicken and die before their very eyes, surrender an ailing child to the nearest orphanage in the hope that it can be saved."

In December 1955, I had paid a visit to an orphanage at Inchon, the port city destroyed in the landings by Allied troops. It was a sprawling brick building pockmarked by war's crossfire and made habitable again through the efforts of work squads of American soldiers. The French Sisters of St. Paul de Chartres, with headdresses like fat white doves, had gathered the children found in the debris of the broken country. One of the sisters was from England, and she was the go-between with the American Army for repairs and building, and a continuous display of charity by the troops.

Though it was almost zero weather, and the Arctic winds whistled through the shaky windows, there was no heat in the building. Improvised heating had been set up in the small room housing the very tiniest of babies. I visited room after room of the older children. There were about four hundred children, every one bundled up warmly in snowsuits and layers of sweaters. They were studying their lessons, and some were practicing carols and chorus singing for Christmas. A choir of little girls stopped their practicing to sing a Korean song called "Shepherd Boy" for me. To my surprise, it turned out to be the old Irish melody "Danny Boy." Imported by Irish missioners to Korea, it had become to all intents and

purposes a Korean folk song. The little voices pierced the icy
air. The cheeks of the youngsters were red and shiny. One
little girl clung to the hand of the Sister who guided me
through the orphanage. She stole shy glances at me but said
nothing. If I drew near to her, she hid her head behind the
apron of the motherly old nun.

"This little girl does not speak at all. She was found after
the bombing in a state of complete shock. All her family were
killed. Who knows what she saw and suffered. Perhaps we
will never find out. But the doctors are working with her.
They give us hope that she will recover her speech. They are
sure she spoke once. Her mind is normal."

The little girl's eyes sparkled as she glanced at me, and I
somehow felt that if there were any chances that she would
speak, it would be in the company of the warmhearted sisters.

I could not put her shy smile out of my mind, nor could I
forget the hundreds of little faces which had turned to me as
I went from room to room of the Inchon orphanage.

Through the Catholic Relief Services Korean Director,
Monsignor George E. Carroll, and Sighle Kennedy, we obtained dossiers of children from a dozen of the most hard-
pressed orphanages. Each dossier contained a picture of the
child with the date of his or her birth and a short personal
description. Miss Margaret Mealey, the Executive Director of
NCCW, Mrs. Elizabeth Zepf, then the NCCW President, and
Mrs. Ulric Scott, Foreign Relief Chairman, presented the
whole plan to the National Council of Catholic Women.
Sponsorship would consist of donating ten dollars monthly to
the child, and keeping in touch through a quarterly exchange
of letters.

Women who had looked with the eyes of compassion on

millions of children in need were now ready to pick a face out of the millions, to whom they could direct a personal love. Hundreds of children found faraway sponsors who would help the orphanage directors to give the children the care of the family they had lost. Each sponsor became a partner in a family effort to make a stable future and a useful, happy life possible for a child in need.

The six-pointed star

Through the works of mercy performed under the six-pointed star of the Foreign Relief Committee, the Catholic women of the United States developed a creative program in cooperation with Catholic Relief Services-N.C.W.C. Through the channel of the bishops' agency, they donated, every year, nearly a million dollars in funds, in gifts, in training opportunities for the homeless, the comfortless, the hungry and the ill around the world. These donations were over and above their annual contributions to the Laetare Sunday collection of the Catholic Bishops Relief Fund.

It is important to emphasize the fact that when American Catholic women turned their attention to overseas needs, they did not cease their work for justice and order at home. In their own communities, they set up services to bring help to migrant workers, to newly arrived Puerto Ricans, to the so-called "Anglos" of New Mexico. Affiliates of NCCW were in the forefront of civil rights activities. When the U.S. government and local communities embarked on the immense war against poverty, the NCCW membership was an integral part of that war. In 1965, in an ecumenical effort of crucial importance to the success of the anti-poverty program, NCCW joined with the United Church Women and the National Council of Jewish Women for planning on a national level and action on the local level. The new grouping was called WICS, Women in Community Service.

The story of international relief which follows cannot in any sense describe the countless numbers of ways in which Christian love went out to comfort helpless sufferers. These chapters can only give the highlights of the results of the cooperative effort of millions of participants.

To those who might question the universality and indiscriminate quality of this work of compassion for the human family, the statement of a social action leader in the Archdiocese of Chicago, Msgr. John J. Egan, provides the Christian response: ". . . Our practices . . . must reflect the totality of our belief in the dignity of man—a dignity which extends to the poor as well as to the minority; a dignity which does not ask, 'What good are you?' or 'What are you?' but a dignity which asks, in fact, no questions at all."

2

Operation Hong Kong

Apostolate of presence

In the waters around the port of Hong Kong are thousands of frail masts rising from sampans and junks which, tiny as they are, form the permanent homes of large Chinese families. Sometimes eight or ten people live on a small boat, sleeping curled up, as the Chinese describe it, like "twisted snakes." They manage to cook their rice aboard the flimsy vessels by watching every spark to see that the wooden slats do not catch fire. Where the boats lie thickest, the bay dwellers make their way to shore by "walking the plank" from one vessel to another.

The fifty thousand people represented by these masts, are the spill-over from the "tight little island" of Hong Kong. After the mainland of China fell to Communist rule, millions fled over the trestle connecting the 2,683,562 square mile nation of China with the 361 square mile colony. The massive exodus began in 1948 and continues today. Three million of the refugees went further and found refuge in Formosa, but about one million remained in Hong Kong, packed into it as into a marooned ship. Clinging desperately around the great ship are the little life rafts of those who could not squeeze aboard.

"Hong Kong is the largest refugee camp in the world," wrote the Rev. Paul Duchesne, Director of the Catholic Relief Services program for refugees and the needy.

One day, Father Duchesne climbed aboard to bless a tiny junk which raised its frail mast among the thousands in the bay and could in no way be picked out from the other boats. But it was different. It was the home of four young girls—two Chinese and two from foreign countries—who were not refugees, but had chosen to become refugees for the sake of Christ. They were members of the Society of the Little Sisters of Jesus.

Realizing that a solution of the massive refugee problem of Hong Kong was beyond human power and certainly beyond any effective help on their part, they decided to make "an apostolate of presence." They formed a team to live among the poorest and most distressed of the exiles, partaking of the same daily struggle, enduring the noise, the dampness, the typhoons. Their presence was a witness to their concern and love. The Little Brothers and the Little Sisters of Jesus, founded by Charles de Foucauld, were first called the Little Nomad Brothers and Sisters when they started their apostolate in the North African desert. As nomads, they identified with the wandering tribes of the Sahara. I met a team in an inaccessible part of Vietnam after the exodus from the north. Other Little Sisters and Little Brothers went to live in prisons to be by the side of those whose condition they could not alter but whose captivity they could assume in their own persons. Here in Hong Kong they identified completely with the life of exile by living it.

Father Duchesne, knowing of their desire for such a life,

found the money to buy the junk, and said Mass on it to start them on their unique way of life. The personal apostolate of presence rests on the apostolate of a sacramental "Presence" and shows how love of neighbor can be exemplified in beautiful and poetic ways in our time.

Another "apostolate of presence" in Hong Kong had been a presence of charity made possible by the Catholic women of the United States. I will cite three examples of its working: The Madonna Plan, NCCW Feed-A-Family, and a rehabilitation project for the refugees known as "Operation Hong Kong."

Morning Star in Hong Kong Bay

The Madonna Plan in Hong Kong was directed to serving the women and children in the junks and sampans. It would take an inventive mind to find a way to bring medical care to sick women who could not even "walk the plank" to come to a doctor on shore. But the Sisters known as Helpers of the Holy Souls have been known for their inventiveness in starting services that no one else would tackle, whether a school for the poor in an Indonesian city, or medical service for the bay dwellers of Hong Kong.

Tsun Wan is on the Kowloon side of Hong Kong, in the heart of an industrial district, overlooking the water-borne city of junks and sampans. Dawn to dark labor was the order of the day, of every day. And even after so much work, Father Duchesne told me, there was sometimes not enough rice to fill the bowl. Nothing was wasted—nothing that the human hand could work over and turn into something useful.

The "tin can factories" were an unforgettable sight. In workshop after little workshop at the bay's edge in Kowloon, I saw men pounding flat every type of tin can, from the small one that had contained peas to the large drum that had carried motor oil. Along one crowded street, there was a line of wooden workshops, each no bigger than a ten foot square room. The incessant pounding was enough to break my eardrums, but the Chinese workmen stayed at their tasks with unbroken tenacity. Out of the pressed-out tin, they made storage bins for rice and flour, each with a good workable lid. They made frying pans and saucepans out of the heavier metals. Candlesticks, wall brackets and ornamental picture-frames were being fashioned before my eyes from used metal that was patiently shined by hand. I asked the price of a frying pan that was just finished. The man looked up just long enough to tell Father Duchesne that it cost two Hong Kong dollars—about thirty-three cents. It was by such labor that the Chinese from the mainland struggled to earn their daily rice. Many of the workers came to the Tsun Wan workshops from the little boats in the bay.

The Helpers of the Holy Souls, a strongly international community, with American, French and Chinese Sisters on the same nursing team, asked for a little site at Tsun Wan to start a clinic for the refugees. They were determined to give special attention to the women and children parked in the waters of the bay. There was literally no building room. Every inch of available land was already crowded with refugees and their workshops, but the government held out a hope. A continual process of filling in land was going on, thus extending the shoreline into what was once water. The Sisters could have enough of this land for their clinic. Shortly after, the first shed-like clinic was erected on the spot, and the Sisters began their visitations to the junks and sampans.

Sister Juliana, an American member of the Helpers of the Holy Souls and a Medical Doctor, came to our office when the medical service was just beginning. We arranged for Sister Juliana to meet Miss Mary Kanane, Relief for Peace Chairman of the Catholic Daughters of America, and out of funds gathered at National Headquarters and sent to our office, the sum of twenty-four hundred dollars was guaranteed for one year. This would allow the Sisters to plan on two hundred dollars a month toward their budget for medicines and milk. This might seem a small sum, but it enabled the Helpers to make their Hong Kong project a going concern.

Help from another source, also a women's overseas aid service, was obtained by Miss Sighle Kennedy, who approached World Medical Relief in Detroit for basic clinic equipment. Mrs. Lester Auberlin, founder of that organization, gathered and reconditioned every type of hospital equipment, from a doctor's examining kit to a complete medical theatre, and sent them around the world—to whatever centers were caring for the sick poor.

Working for the poor without reference to race, creed or religion, Mrs. Auberlin was ready and able to supply the clinic at Tsun Wan such needs as the Sisters specified. Though they only had a shed on a filled-in piece of land, they knew that somehow they would find a way to erect a really practical clinic—one that would include a special wing for ailing children.

At that point Providence entered in an extraordinary way. American Government officials in Hong Kong were informed that they could recommend certain refugee aid projects for special grants to be made from funds set aside by the United States for World Refugee Year. Monsignor John Romaniello, the Maryknoll priest who replaced Father Duchesne as Catholic Relief Services delegate in Hong Kong, called attention to the work of the Sisters at Tsun Wan. The Helpers of the

Holy Souls, scurrying about the tiny refugee homes of Tsun Wan, and ferrying around the bay, came under the scrutiny of men who could make their dream of a real clinic possible.

In short order a Refugee Year grant went to the "Helpers" allowing for the erection of a four story clinic, with the hoped-for children's wing. On May 5, 1960, the hospital-clinic was dedicated by the Consul General of the United States in Hong Kong. Also present was the Assistant Executive Director of Catholic Relief Services-N.C.W.C., Monsignor John F. McCarthy, and the Far East Director of the agency, Monsignor Joseph J. Harnett. On a world tour to see refugees' and other needs, they stopped in Hong Kong just in time to help inaugurate the new medical service, christened The Morning Star Hospital-Clinic. It brought light and hope to thousands of families, especially to mothers and children, in want and in pain. Support from the Madonna Plan continued, supplying the items that could not be obtained from other sources, in one case a sterilizer for the laboratory of the clinic-hospital.

Operation Hong Kong

Many homes in the United States possess tangible reminders of the skills of Hong Kong's refugees in the form of hand-fashioned Chinese dolls. The most popular of these dolls was a Chinese mother with her baby, a separate tiny doll, strapped to her back by a little blanket.

The dolls were made by refugees, many of them women who were the chief support of their children. Some gathered in workshops while others got the materials at a central depot and took them home for painting and sewing while they kept an eye on their youngsters.

The connection between the doll makers in Hong Kong and buyers in the United States was an American woman, Mrs. Arthur L. Zepf, who, while serving as Foreign Relief Chairman for the NCCW, spent some time at our New York Headquarters. Elizabeth Zepf was a native of Cincinnati, the wife of an insurance executive who was as interested in the Foreign Relief Committee's work as she was herself. For four years, before she was elected National President of the NCCW, she tirelessly promoted every aspect of the NCCW overseas aid effort.

When Mrs. Zepf arrived in New York, we had just received samples of handcrafted dolls from Hong Kong, produced through a rehabilitation effort known as the China Refugee Development Organization, which was trying to find outlets for the dolls sitting in our office.

As a voluntary, non-profit agency, we did not want to get into the problem of marketing—even the marketing of refugee handicrafts, but Elizabeth Zepf was delighted with the eleven-inch dolls and the delicate, removable garments of brocade handwoven by Chinese women. "This is a program that we women should be doing," she exclaimed. "If we cannot sell the dolls through headquarters, I'll sell them from my own home."

Mrs. Zepf's only son was away at college, and she had the time and the heart to assume heavy burdens, but it proved unnecessary to do the work from her own house. The National Headquarters accepted the new program on behalf of the Chinese in Hong Kong. Five out of the dozen doll models were selected as the most saleable—Mother and Child, Bride, Court Lady, Country Girl and Country Boy.

Mrs. Zepf, in her talks before women's diocesan councils, always had a set of dolls with her. She described the needs of

Hong Kong and a special leaflet, "Operation China Doll," was prepared giving a résumé of the situation there. Pictures of women making the dolls, photographs of different doll models, and order blanks, completed the leaflet.

Orders began coming in to the Washington office of NCCW and were speeded to the Hong Kong office of Catholic Relief Services-N.C.W.C. Hundreds of refugees were given work to fill the orders. Though at first it was feasible to have the dolls sent directly to the buyers from Hong Kong, it was later decided to speed delivery by stocking them at the warehouse of Catholic Relief Services in the Bronx.

During World Refugee Year, from July 1, 1959 to June 30, 1960, the dolls were placed on display in a pavilion in Geneva, Switzerland, devoted to World Refugee Year. When a new high peak of sales was registered in 1960, a second product was ordered from the Hong Kong refugees, a brocade woman's travel or jewelry bag called the Mandarin Bag. All this was included in "Operation Hong Kong," and each article sold fed the relief programs for Hong Kong by reminding the U.S. that the refugees from the mainland were still clinging precariously to life on the edge of the Bamboo Curtain.

I am here as a stranger

When all efforts to find work failed them, the refugees of Hong Kong sat by the wayside and begged for alms. They might have been people of means in China's hinterland, professional men, journalists, teachers, government officials; they might have been simple peasants or ex-soldiers. One of the most heart-stopping sights in Hong Kong was to see a dignified man squatting on the sidewalk waiting for the casual alms of the passers-by. In order to establish his credentials to beg he would spread before him on the street a piece of paper with his story carefully painted in Chinese characters.

We received pictures of such beggars from our Hong Kong office. One showed a refugee mother holding a child wrapped in a blanket. By her side was a wicker basket containing her worldly possessions. Before her was a large piece of paper, torn at the edges. In large characters, so that it could be read without difficulty, was the bitter story already written on her face and in her heart. Stella Huang, a Chinese girl who had worked with our office in Hong Kong, picked up the picture and began translating the woman's story for us.

"I am a refugee women, Chen Hou," she read. "I am here as a stranger and have no home and no place to go. I have five members in my family. As a grown-up I can endure hunger— but the children have to have something to feed them. I ask you to show your sympathy and to help me with your generosity."

It was for such families as this woman's, exiled and helpless, that the Feed-A-Family program was extended to Hong Kong by the National Council of Catholic Women.

In an economy where one American dollar was worth six Hong Kong dollars, and where a five dollar Feed-A-Family gift became transmitted into many times its value, the NCCW effort was literally a life-saver. It was first thought that the food packages would be made up in New York and shipped to the Field Mission Director in Hong Kong, Father Paul Duchesne, for distribution through his network of charity. This proved impractical, and Father Duchesne wrote that if we sent the money directly to him, he could arrange to have the packages made up locally. It turned out that this arrangement was a far better bargain than any package we could have had made up in the United States. Much more to the taste of the refugees were prized local foods like cooking oil, beans, dried vegetables and dried fish.

Father Duchesne described the program in an article entitled, "Miracles of Charity in the Hong Kong Hills."

"Most warmhearted of all our refugee projects," he stated, "is one started by the National Council of Catholic Women— the Hong Kong Feed-A-Family program. So successful has this proved in action that I keep hoping some miracle will multiply it a thousandfold. Hundreds of American men, women—and children too—have 'adopted' destitute refugee families here by providing food packages for them several times a year. Each five dollars in U.S. money, forwarded to us through our central Catholic Relief office in New York City is multiplied to a value of fifteen dollars in purchasing power in Hong Kong. Packages supplementing a hungry family's diet for almost a month can be assembled for that amount. . . . Each family package contains about fifty pounds of the foods most wanted in everyday Chinese life; twenty-eight pounds of rice; four pounds of dried meat, or fish; six pounds of beans; four pounds of dried vegetables; and two quart-bottles of cooking oil. These foods not only are the most nutritious available—but they are the best adapted for storage in refugee huts, which give practically no protection from rain or heat.

"In a simple and direct fashion our Feed-A-Family program demonstrates one of the most joyful fruits of our faith— that all men are truly brothers in Christ. With its help I see miracles of charity take place on our Hong Kong hills every day—a generous New Jersey housewife takes under her wing a Chinese grandmother who runs a ferry all day, supporting three sickly grandchildren and an invalid daughter. A young pipefitter from Chicago saves the family of a fellow-fitter starving in a Hong Kong attic and builds a new house for them."

When I visited Hong Kong in December 1955, I went up to one of the squatter cities that climb the nineteen hills along the coastal strip. My guide was a tall, outgoing Maryknoll Sister from the U.S. The hill was like the prow of an old ship completely covered by barnacles—the barnacles in this case being the shanties patched together from every kind of oddment—from cardboard and canvas to the omnipresent flattened tin can. They clung to every piece of exposed land in every imaginable position, some lopsided, looking ready to careen downhill. It was the dry season, otherwise the tiny irregular dirt path that we were treading would have been a muddy rivulet.

We were going to visit one of the families aided by the Feed-A-Family program. They were waiting for us in a hut made of old boards that looked like an enlarged packing case. It was an even square, in contrast to the other huts. The father, pale and consumptive looking, was unemployed. He had been a farmer in Kwantung Province and had been in exile over five years. The mother and five children sat on the one piece of furniture in the hut—a large slatted wooden bench that served as seat, table and at night as bed.

The mother's expression did not change while she gave the news to Sister that one of her children had died. It was one of the many occasions I had to note the utter control and courtesy of the Chinese. It was not good form to weep in front of anyone or to burden others with their tragedies.

As we left I remarked that these must be the poorest of the poor. We were passing shanties made in every conceivable shape, with walls pieced together of any available material. "No," said Sister. "These are a step higher than the poorest of the poor. We consider the sidewalk dwellers the very poorest. They stretch out a piece of canvas on the pavement, and sleep right out in the open. Others find more or less secluded nooks, and string up pieces of cloth and canvas over them. The weather is pretty nice now, though it is cold at night. But when the rains and the typhoons come, it is dreadful for them. No wonder over eighty percent of the refugees have T.B. in some form or other. You can see why we worked so hard to experiment with cheap housing."

The achievement of constructing one room homes with tiny kitchens, out of local stone and cement, could be largely credited to the Maryknoll Sisters. After seeing disastrous fires sweep up and down the squatter cities on the hills, making the refugees doubly homeless, they decided to tackle on a tiny scale the problem of housing the homeless.

Sister showed me their first refugee housing development of sixty-four houses. I looked over the one-room dwellings, clean and secure, typhoon-proof as well as fireproof, and I saw the teeming family life going on in order and security. The cottages were painted a clear white and lent the life of exile a peace and dignity tragically lacking in the rabbit warren shelters of the nearby hills. Our agency had supported this housing experiment with a grant of ten thousand dollars.

A family that had received Feed-A-Family aid was in the midst of moving into their newly completed house. Mr. Leung was an ex-soldier of the Nationalist Army who had been in Hong Kong since 1949. Two years after he arrived, his hut was among those burnt down when a spark from a cooking fire destroyed the homes of sixteen thousand refugees from the mainland. For four and a half years, Leung and his family had been living on the streets. Mrs. Leung tried to smile, but her face was grey and exhausted. The children, one three years old and the other a baby of three months, were bundled up and sitting on the floor among the wicker baskets, the pieces of canvas, and the boxes of buttons. Leung was a man in his thirties, but the fight to keep himself and his family alive had clawed lines of age into his face.

"How much are you earning these days?" asked Father Duchesne. "Are things any better for you?"

"Well, with this house, yes." His face relaxed as he gazed at the four bare walls of his ten foot square home. "But today and yesterday, I have only completed six pounds of buttons." His job, done "at home" on the sidewalk, consisted of clipping the imperfections from plastic buttons. "They give me thirty-five cents for two pounds."

Father Duchesne explained. "That means that in two days Leung has earned a bit more than one Hong Kong dollar. He can buy little more than two pounds of middle grade rice. Maybe the excitement of moving has slowed his work down."

We decided then and there that Leung and his family should be continued on the Feed-A-Family list. We wished them well and left them to the opening of the wicker baskets. But as we walked away, Mr. and Mrs. Leung came and stood in their doorway with a quiet pride.

Father Duchesne's attitude toward the people we visited that day proved something to me. In the enormous tasks of administering a feeding program as well as millions of pounds of clothing and special medicines, Father did not forget the individual and his unique problems. Hong Kong was his parish, and he had never lost the joy of being a pastor from the time he was given the spiritual charge of a parish in Canton, in southern China. Hong Kong was as much exile for him as it was for the Chinese refugees who had converged on it from all parts of China.

Keys to the mystery of survival

The program of Catholic Relief Services in Hong Kong, which grew larger each year as more surplus foods and wearable clothing became available, would not have been the effective instrument of life-preservation that it was had not many other exiles from China participated in it. As Chinese priests and Sisters, and European and American missioners were forced to leave China, they decided to camp on the mainland's doorstep and minister to its refugees. The religious from other countries could have returned to them, secure in the knowledge that they had done what they could for China while the country was open to them. Worn out as many were by imprisonment and false trials before Peoples' Tribunals, these men and women felt that the Chinese, in their homelessness and hopelessness, had a greater call on them than ever before. They settled in Hong Kong, Formosa and Macao for a corporate labor as heroic and as fruitful as anything the Church had seen in its long history.

In Hong Kong, close to forty religious orders were working among the refugees. There were almost a thousand priests, brothers and sisters representing thirty-five different nations, including the United States, Canada, Spain, Italy, France, Germany, Belgium, Holland, Portugal, Poland, Ireland and Australia. The monumental work of the Maryknoll Sisters and Fathers was buttressed, of course, by the resources of a prosperous nation. For example, when Cardinal Spellman saw how effectively a Maryknoll welfare center met the needs of the poor refugees, he gave them funds for the erection of nine such centers in the most crowded refugee sections of the colony. One could not catalogue the nearly two hundred dispensaries, clinics, schools, and training centers operated by missioners expelled from the interior of China.

The Tang King Po School of the Salesian Fathers and Brothers taught useful trades to thousands of Chinese orphans and refugee children. The series of books entitled "Catechetical Scenes," which teach the truths of the Christian faith with the aid of artistic stand-up cut-outs as well as text, could only have been printed by people as skilled and industrious as the Chinese. Through the Rev. Arthur Dempsey, the Pius XII Handicrafts School received U.S. Government grants for refugee training courses, and the products of this school have been sent all around the world. Dedicated men and women representing many Christian groups of Europe and North America set up a variety of welfare services too numerous to catalogue. These services were superimposed on such Chinese efforts as the Free China Relief Society.

The existence of a labyrinthine network of the works of mercy gave one of the keys to the miraculous survival of more than a million newcomers, mostly destitute, in a small rocky island and a tiny territory, together less than four hundred square miles. The miracle is related to the compassion and charity of men and women of many nations, especially those whose life mission was to China. This compassion and charity were expended in marvelous and creative ways on behalf of some of the bravest and most hard-working people the world has ever known—the Chinese refugees.

Thirst for living water

One of the problems of Hong Kong, which had intermittently plagued the colony for a hundred years, was that of drinking water. A few drought years, occurring a decade after the first great refugee exodus, brought the three and a half million community to utter crisis. Rationing became more and more stringent until for months at a time water taps flowed for only four hours every fourth day. This was serious enough in private homes, but catastrophic for the refugees who had to depend on public water taps.

Despite all efforts at storing and family rationing, infants and children in the crowded refugee settlements were the special victims of the water failure. But somehow Hong Kong's population survived. Hundreds stood in line before each community tap during the precious hours when cans and buckets could be filled. Riots broke out among the desperate people in the almost endless queues. At the end of a hand-to-hand struggle between two women, one of them threw a bucket of water in the face of the other. She was arrested, not for disturbing the peace, but for wasting the precious water. Fortunately, the pipeline from Kwangtung Province on the mainland continued to flow. In addition, a fleet of tankers journeyed daily up the Pearl River in Communist China to bring back supplies of potable water.

While water was gratefully received from the mainland, a new influx of refugees had to be refused. The second exodus began to build up in the spring of 1962, when the steady trickle of refugees suddenly became a flood which burst over the border into the area known as the New Territories. Such a flood might threaten those who had already found asylum in the colony.

Wave after wave of escapees were gathered into the Fan Ling transit camp just inside the border. The newcomers were famished. Many reported that they were city people, drawn from the towns of south China. When the harvest threatened to fail, they were shunted in droves to the collective farms of the vast countryside. The harvests did fail, disastrously, and the already uprooted people turned their steps to Hong Kong. Some of the escapees wanted no more than a supply of food; others wanted to be received as permanent refugees.

Bishop Edward E. Swanstrom, Director of Catholic Relief Services, then surveying relief programs in the Orient, interrupted his tour to go in person to Fan Ling. He joined with other churches' overseas aid leaders, including Hugh Farley, Director of Church World Service, and Pastor Ludwig Stumpf of Lutheran World Relief in Hong Kong, in an appeal to the government of the United States to accept new Chinese refugees as immigrants. The highest number that American authorities were prepared to allow in was a total of ten thousand from among those registered in Hong Kong. Meanwhile, Fan Ling was being filled and emptied over and over again as the refugees were fed and sent back over the border into their homeland.

A photographer captured a symbolic scene of one young escapee just before she was placed on the truck for the journey to the border. She was barefoot, and was photographed as she crumpled helplessly to the ground. She was sobbing into a torn rag that served her as handkerchief. The journalist found out that she was nineteen years old and that her name was Lee Ying.

Her picture went around the world. In her small person was concentrated the anguish of the nearly one hundred thousand people whom hunger had driven to desperate measures, and who had knocked on the door of a colony already bursting with people who had to battle daily with hunger and thirst.

Most of the Chinese massed in the fields and woodlands behind the line of demarcation had walked long miles to arrive at this point. But some escapees, by boat or by swimming, made their way across a more difficult and perilous route—a channel of water that washed the shore of the tiny colony of Macao near Hong Kong. Soon they were arriving at the rate of three hundred a day into a remnant of the Portuguese imperial holdings in the Orient.

Through Macao's Casa Ricci, Feed-A-Family parcels had been given out over a long period to the most destitute of the refugees. The Casa Ricci charity center, named for an Italian Franciscan who had entered China in the sixteenth century, gave first aid of all kinds to the newcomers. The team of Jesuit priests at the center sent out a cry for help in the spring of 1962. They had no more room in the shelter and wanted to keep alive the weakened Chinese who were forced to sleep out on the streets.

At that moment, the funds received from the sale of Feed-A-Family Christmas cards were received at Catholic Relief Services from the headquarters of NCCW, and this money was cabled to Macao. It was enough to provide quilts for nearly all the escapees who reached the colony's shores during that desperate spring. Even if their first sleeping quarters were arcades in the streets, they would not be allowed to perish of exposure. Even when Macao, only six and a half miles square, could no longer find any space for the refugees, they were not pushed away from its beaches. The newcomers were transferred to nearby islands, Coloane, Green Island and Taipa.

These islands were really the end of the line for those who had managed to escape. They might easily have thought that the world had forgotten them. But the Catholic Relief Services representative in Macao, the Reverend Lancelot Rodriquez, followed them even to the sequestered havens. To

Coloane he took part of a shipment of twenty thousand new garments donated at the convention of the Winona Diocesan Council of Catholic Women. The moderator of this group, Monsignor Richard Feiten, had visited Macao on a tour of Catholic Relief Services' Asian programs led by Monsignor Joseph Harnett, the agency's Far East Director. Monsignor Feiten and the Winona women wished to have their gifts directed to Macao.

New China and old faith

There are some things, however, that could not be viewed with the naked eye or seen in a camera lens—mysteries of grace and suffering, for example. There was a tremendous up-swell of Christianity in the Chinese diaspora. All Christian groups felt it. Perhaps the shock that the refugees had ex-perienced in losing everything had made them open to new values. Perhaps the emptiness and precariousness of their lives drove them to an avid search for final answers. Perhaps because they saw Christianity at its best—in the form of uni-versal charity—at their lowest moments, they moved toward the acceptance of Christian dogma.

Perhaps it was all of these factors plus the effect of what had happened and was happening in China. Christians are told that the blood of martyrs serves as the germinating seed from which the Chrisian faith grows, and looking into China from Hong Kong, one sees a vast land of countless martyr-doms. The imprisonments, torturings and expulsions of European and American Christians have been told in the world press. The long and terrible persecution of the Chinese Christians is less known.

One could not leave the story of the Chinese refugees with-out telling two examples of Chinese Catholics who refused to leave their homeland. They upheld Christianity against an all-powerful state, and by their example inspired their own people and can inspire Christians of the whole world.

One story was brought out of Shanghai by a Canadian priest who was a member of the staff of Catholic Relief Services. Kept under house arrest and questioned continuously for a period of years, he nevertheless had a chance to see the new China at work. He told us of the heroism of Chinese girls at a time when special "political teachers" were installed in the Catholic schools and colleges. The Legion of Mary, an organization of women for spreading and strengthening the Catholic faith, was very active in three Catholic girls high schools and two women's colleges in Shanghai. The political propagandists directed their attention to the Legion, and devised a plan whereby girls associated with the organization would sign a statement against it. The statement averred simply that the Legion of Mary was subversive to the new government of China, was a criminal organization and anti-revolutionary in character. New China wanted only Communist leaders; the Legion became a focus of attack because it produced leaders opposed to the new system.

Many of the Catholic girls were converts, sometimes from non-Christian families. The political activists visited their parents, asking them to urge their daughters to sign this convenient paper, and thus consolidate the family's position with the regime. If the girl failed to sign, her whole family, as well as she herself, might suffer serious political and economic difficulties, since her refusal would be considered a sign of political disaffection.

During their school hours, and in their free time at home, these young girls were pressed for hours on end to sign the statement. They were threatened with jail and torture, and were given a deadline by which they were expected to sign. The authorities seemed to expect that high school girls would fall into line very easily.

At the same time great numbers of Catholics in the city of Shanghai were asked to sign the Pledge of the Three Autonomies. This called for signed assent to three autonomies for the Catholic Church in China: the Church should be completely independent, completely self-supporting, and entirely Chinese. The members of the Legion of Mary, as a Catholic Action group, had been tireless in strengthening hard-pressed people in their resistance to the Three Autonomies petition, pointing out that it really meant a national church separated from the Holy See.

The resistance to the pledge surprised the propagandists, but what surprised them more was their utter inability to cajole, threaten, torture or force young girls into signing the anti-Legion of Mary statement. These girls, often recently baptized, realized that by signing against the Legion they would be in effect abjuring their faith.

As the deadline approached, a surprising thing happened. More and more of the girls, Legion members and auxiliaries, came to school with their hair cut short like boys, and carrying in their arms a bundle of clothing or a small valise from which they refused to be parted. Finally on the last day, hundreds came to school in this fashion. When they were asked the reason, these girls explained that they were definitely not going to sign away their faith. The Legion of Mary was not subversive or criminal, and their Catholic faith was not a political matter. They had been told that refusal to sign would probably mean jail. Women in jail had their hair cut short. They were ready to go to jail at any time, and with their little valise or bundle could go right from school if the "political teachers" ordered it. Many of these young women were sentenced to long jail terms for their steadfastness of faith.

Another example of Chinese fortitude which should be better known concerns a Chinese priest of Shanghai who could only oppose the false teaching of the Three Autonomies by choosing death. He was Father John Tung, who worked at the Catholic Central Bureau. He was called upon by the authorities to talk before a large group of Chinese Catholics forcibly brought together in Chungking; the object of his speech, to win the captive audience over to the idea of an independent, that is, Chinese, Church, a church under the iron thumb of a political regime. Father Tung agreed to speak and he appeared on the platform with the full approval of the Communist officials. This soon turned to dismay. Father Tung delivered a speech that would in all probability mean his death, because in it he flaunted his opposition to the totalitarian authority of the state.

He began:

"In the Name of the Father, and of the Son, and of the Holy Ghost. Amen. Most Sacred Heart of Jesus, have mercy on us. Holy Apostles Peter and Paul, pray for us.

"Authorities of the Government, dignitaries of the Church, Christians who are loyal to your faith, and gentlemen. The subject of this speech will be: the sacrifice that I make of myself to the two supreme powers, my religion and the state.

"Some persons who do not believe in the existence of God, nor in the existence of the soul, who do not recognize the Pope as being the representative of Christ, who do not recognize the Catholic hierarchy, present the Triple Autonomy Movement as a purely patriotic movement. These same persons recognize the liberty to adhere to the Catholic faith; they admit that purely spiritual relations may exist between the faithful and the Pope. But a movement which has evolved outside the hierarchy, today invites us to attack the representative of the Pope, His Excellency, Msgr. Riberi. Tomorrow we perhaps shall be asked to attack the Pope himself, who is Christ's representative. Why, the day after tomorrow, should we not be asked to attack Our Lord and God, Jesus Christ himself? We may always, in the course of an attack, make distinctions. But in reality, God is 'one' and the Pope's representative is 'one' and the Pope himself is 'one.' No distinction, no division is admissible. Such a development—the Triple Independence—would take from me all possibility of remaining a Catholic. A patriotic movement of such a nature is in fact incompatible with the Catholic Church.

"Gentlemen, I have only one soul and I cannot divide it. I have a body which can be divided. It is best, it seems, to offer my whole soul to God and to the Holy Church; and my body to my country. If she is pleased with it, I do not refuse it to her. Good materialists who deny the existence of the soul, cannot but be satisfied with the offering of my body only. I believe that if the state and the Church could collaborate, the movement for Triple Autonomy, conformable to Catholic principles, would be recognized as a patriotic movement. If it were so, how much good would result both for the State and for the Church! But on the contrary, the more the movement progresses the farther one is from the other. We have reached a point where almost any backward step is impossible. Very soon, the last thread to which we can attach our hope will be broken."

Later in his talk he paid a tribute to the Communists that might well have given them pause:

"It is true that I am a Catholic. But this does not prevent me from having a very great admiration for the Communists. They believe neither in God nor in the soul, still less in heaven or hell. It is my conviction that they are mistaken. However, they have more than one quality which compels admiration, shakes my own indolence and brings me to recall vividly the countless martyrs of our Church during the course of 2,000 years. These martyrs are the ones who urge me to beseech God, day and night, to forgive my numerous sins and grant me the unparalleled gift of martyrdom.

"The first admirable quality of the Communists is that they are capable of facing death. They never betray their cause and deceive others by giving some excuse, as General Li Ling did to rationalize his capitulation: 'If I did not fight to death, it is because I was preserving myself for future deeds.' Should I a Catholic be cowardly, or attached to life, and use the pretext of preserving myself for future service to the Church? A Christian who betrays his God also betrays his Church and his country. The Communists are wont to say: 'For one who falls, 10,000 will rise.' How could a Catholic forget: 'the blood of martyrs is the seed of Christians'?"

Father Tung's offer of his life was clearly for the souls of his people:

"I do not content myself with admiring the unshakable courage of the Communists, and thank them for their noble intention of trying to win the Christians. I still have a great desire. It is to offer them the Catholic Church which is so dear to me, in order to bring them to God and make them our brothers in the faith. Do not say I am a fool who prattles crazy things, and do not believe that I lack sincerity! I dare say that Communists who have a high ideal would make good Catholics completely devoted to their faith and would surpass a thousand times a Catholic such as I am, when the day dawns that they really know the Catholic Church. I also ask God that in the Communist Party there may be found many Sauls to become Pauls, who will far surpass the poor priest that I am. It is my most fervent prayer. To this end, I spare myself no sacrifice, praying with hope that the earthly life which I offer today might bring the conversion of future generations. . . .

"I am a Catholic Chinese. I love my country but I also love my Church. I categorically disapprove of anything that is in opposition to the laws of my country or to the laws of my Church, and before all I strongly refuse anything that could breed discord. But if the Church and the government can't achieve an accord, all Chinese Catholics, sooner or later, will have only to die. Why not then immediately offer my life to hasten the mutual understanding of both parties?"

After his offering of self as the victim for the reconciliation between man and man, as his Master had given himself as victim for the reconciliation of man to God, Father Tung drew his speech to a close. He hoped that the peace offering of himself would not be rejected, and that the Government would be moved to call a halt before it permitted itself to be drawn into a position of demanding the death of China's faithful Catholics.

As he finished his speech, Father John Tung was led away. The date was July 5, 1951. Nothing was ever heard from him again.

Hong Kong could not be understood without taking into account such spiritual triumphs as those that occurred in the Christian communities of Shanghai, Chungking, and other cities, towns and villages in the new China.

3

Mother Teresa opens a window on the world

Las Vegas

One of the side effects, though not the least important aspect, of the Foreign Relief Committee program of the NCCW was to provide a window opening on the world, which allowed those in the smallest communities of the United States to look beyond their immediate concerns and to view the drama of the world at large. Sister Regereau had brought the drama of the beginnings of Catholic overseas aid to the twenty-third National Convention, and the thirtieth Convention at Las Vegas seemed an opportune time to demonstrate the role of Catholic relief in Asia. Mother Teresa, through whose hands large amounts of Catholic aid, including Madonna Plan help, had been channeled to India's poorest, was the voice of Asia's need and of Asia's dignity.

The convention took place in the month of October when Nevada was sunlit but bracingly cool and dry. The pleasure and gambling empire carved out of the desert was in swinging activity night and day. On the wide highway known as

"The Strip," the hotels offered their luxuries around the clock—open-air swimming pools, lobbies filled with clunking slot machines and spinning roulette wheels. Fabulous midnight feasts featured giant roasts of beef as well as fish and lobster flown in from the California coast.

In downtown Las Vegas, the main street was so festooned with thousands of electric bulbs that it was referred to as "Glitter Gulch." Its nightclubs offered the plush atmosphere of the Gay Nineties or a reminder of frontier life. On "Glitter Gulch," as on "The Strip," were a series of small wooden chapels, so tiny they looked like toy churches for a miniature play village. Bright signs hung from their neon-lit steeples and windows:

> Weddings—Complete with Corsage—Fifteen Dollars—Any Time of Day or Night.

The city fathers had offered the NCCW free use of a great horseshoe-shaped hall for its thirtieth biennial meeting, and the Las Vegas offer was accepted.

For a gruelling four days, the women lived at hotels and tourist homes throughout the city, and traveled by bus, taxi and car to Mass in the Convention Hall's great auditorium. After the early morning liturgy, they separated and went off to meetings, panel discussions and workshops which went on continually through the mornings, afternoons and evenings.

In the Convention Exhibit Hall were booths, many home-made, showing the activities of the seventeen national committees of the NCCW—the services to migrant workers from Mexico, hospitality and help to Displaced Persons and foreign students, Civil Defense, Home and School Associations,

Rural Life, and other committees concerned with Christian living and spiritual development.

Several booths featured the involvement of American Catholic women with people and problems outside the borders of the United States. These included the booths illustrating the work of the committees on International Relations, Inter-American Relations and Foreign Relief. At the Foreign Relief booth, which was staffed by volunteers recruited by Mrs. Ulric Scott, volunteer National Chairman of that committee, were displayed graphic scenes of refugee life in Hong Kong; in front of these Chinese handicrafts were placed for sale. There were pictures of refugees and the needy from Calcutta, Seoul, Santiago, Saigon. A new piece of literature prepared by Catholic Relief Services told of Madonna Plan aid around the world, and was given out gratis.

At times Mother Teresa sat at the booth. At these times, women delegates flocked to the display, putting question after question to the woman in the white, blue-bordered sari. Many were surprised to learn that she was not a native Indian. With her tanned skin and brown eyes, she could easily have been taken for a woman of the Punjab. They asked about her origins in Skopje, Yugoslavia, about her reasons for becoming an Indian citizen, about the use of the sari as a habit. Interest was strong in the Missionaries of Charity, the congregation she had founded.

The woman whose dress was so unusual that she was dubbed "Mahatma Gandhi" by one of the leaders of the Convention, must have been one of the strangest visitors ever to arrive in Las Vegas. Surrounded by unparalleled opulence was a woman who had made poverty a central guideline of her life—a Franciscan poverty which delighted in divesting itself of created things the better to serve the poorest creatures of God. Mother Teresa was only one of many outstanding speakers and panelists at the Las Vegas Convention, but she was probably the one who made the greatest impact on those attending.

Though a reluctant speaker who had never made a formal, public speech before, she agreed to come to the United States to talk to the whole assemblage of delegates at a morning meeting. For three afternoons, she participated in a workshop panel of the Foreign Relief Committee. At other times she spoke privately to women who wanted to meet her, or sat at the Foreign Relief Committee booth, ready to answer any questions addressed to her.

In 1958 I had spent nearly three months in Calcutta, as a staff member of Catholic Relief Services, close to Mother Teresa's work in a great city where all the problems of Asia are concentrated in heart-rending intensity. Our agency was the channel through which U.S. surplus food reached the hungry of India.

I had seen Mother Teresa's answers to these problems—answers arrived at with the cooperation of the Indian community and of city and provincial governmental agencies. These answers included a Home for the dying, fourteen free schools in the poorest slums, six mother and child clinics, the Holy Family Clinic for healthy babies, a Home for crippled and abandoned children, eight treatment stations for lepers. As more young women were drawn to the Missionaries of Charity, one or more of these services was opened in towns all over India—Delhi, Agra, Bombay, Simla, Ranchi, Trivandrum and Jhansi.

In all her talks with the delegates, Mother Teresa opened the window on world needs wider than it had ever been before. If any of the delegates had had the slightest temptation to accept uncritically a materialist or pleasure-oriented view of life, divorced from sacrifice and the works of mercy, Mother Teresa's words buttressed their higher nature.

Standing before them in a sari that cost less than a dollar, wearing the rough leather sandals of the poor, she told them of the daily work of the Missionaries of Charity. A new order, vowed to "wholehearted free service to the poorest of the poor," it chose as the first recipients of its aid the homeless of Calcutta. The capital of Bengal, a refugee-packed city in a refugee-filled province, could not call on any resources sufficient to meet the needs of the near-million destitute newcomers who clung to life in its *bustees,* or slums. Even those who had some kind of shelter, such as a rented room or hut, were perilously close to the street if they fell on illness or unemployment. One of the city's most tragic problems was that of the destitute people who were put out on the streets to die. Only when they had breathed their last were they picked up—to be taken to the funeral pyres near a tributary of the holy Ganges River.

When Mother Teresa offered her Missionaries of Charity for the work of providing a decent human death for those otherwise left to die like animals in the open streets, the Corporation of Calcutta made the pilgrim's hostel in the compound of the famous temple of Kali available to them. To the hostel, in south Calcutta, ambulances brought the men and women, sometimes children, found dying alone on the dusty streets.

In simple terms, Mother Teresa told of how these poor were given the love and respect due every human being. Some survived and needed help to start a renewed life. Some were already beyond all aid, but at least the reassurance of a loving human concern was given to them.

In thanking the affiliates of the NCCW who had sent money halfway around the world for the families in her care and for her mother and child clinics, she gave her listeners a picture of the trials and courage of Indian women. She brought a greeting from the woman Governor of the Bengal Province, Padmaji Naidu, daughter of a great woman poet and associate of Gandhi. Mother Teresa cited as examples of India's contemporary women the girls who had joined her congregation. They represented the varied languages and castes of the Indian continent. Their heroism in serving the dying, the lepers, the homeless, the hungry, the ill of an afflicted city, she told us, was strengthened by the help and understanding they received from the women of the United States.

She gave examples of the courage of the women of India who had received aid from American Catholic women. Need was the only requisite for this aid.

"Two or three weeks back, before I came here," she said, "a woman suffering in the last stages of T.B. came with her little son, Jamal. Jamal is a Mohammedan name. When I went there she only asked: 'Mother, as I have got a terrible disease and my days are counted, take my child, give him a home, love him.' I took the child and I told her: 'Well, as long as you are alive, come twice or three times a day, if you like, and see the child. I will keep the child with me as long as you are alive.' And there was this woman walking at least two or three miles every day, and she loved the child in such an heroic way. She would not touch him and begged me: 'Mother, take my child in your arms; you love him and by seeing you love him, that will give me pleasure. Because if I touch the child I may give him the disease.' This is what your help has done for Indian mothers. It has helped the Sisters to draw out of those good mothers the best in them."

Sister Teresa went on: "We in India love our children. The mothers, as poor as they may be, as sick as they may be—cling to their children. A leper woman living far away from Titaghur, one of our leper centers, had heard that the Sisters were taking care of the leper patients. She had it herself, and she had a little child of two, Bhakti was her name. Bhakti means love. She walked miles to the clinic just to make sure that her little Bhakti didn't have the disease. She thought that she saw on her body a white spot, the sign of the disease. And though her feet were partly eaten away, and her hands were without fingers, still this brave woman, this loving woman, carried the child all the way for several miles to the Sisters to make sure that her child did not have leprosy. And when Sister examined her and found that the child was safe, she was so happy she was not afraid to walk back all the way! If you think the mothers don't care for their children in India, after an example like this, I don't know what to say. And examples such as these happen daily and the joy and the happiness these people feel—it is you who shared in it."

After Mother Teresa's talk, the combined unsolicited gifts totalled several thousand dollars. But even more important than what the women delegates gave was what they took away. Their window on the world had been opened by Mother Teresa and other speakers, experts in many fields. These delegates would fan out after the meeting to every state in the Union. They would first give their reports to the Diocesan Councils of Catholic Women and later these reports on the Convention would be studied at meetings of groups of parishes (called deaneries). Finally, the women of the individual parish, the cell of Christian life, would receive the message and decide how they could put into action the knowledge received at Las Vegas. In one way or another, the words pronounced there would go out to touch the lives of some nine million American women. What the women from Alaska or New York did as a result of these words was decided by the local organizations.

At Las Vegas I became very much aware of how a person can be in a place and not of it, as the Christian is supposed to be in the world but not a part of it. Mother Teresa saw the gaiety, the gambling, the great clusters of lights of the Las Vegas landscape on her way to talks at the Convention Hall. I asked her what she thought of this phenomenon and she answered as only an Indian would.

I knew that in India there is a yearly festival of lights, called Dewali, a time of great joy because it commemorates the return of the god Rama from Ceylon with his beloved Sita who had been abducted. Towns and villages blossom with candles and strings of electric bulbs.

In answer to my question about Las Vegas, Mother Teresa looked around, smiled, and said one word—"Dewali." She made no moral pronouncements, cast no aspersions on the gambling and merrymaking that was such a costly proposition that its proceeds would have fed many of Calcutta's hungry. Being only in Las Vegas, and not of it in any sense of the term, it had probably never occurred to Mother Teresa that Las Vegas was almost a way of life for some people. A perpetual "Dewali" would be unthinkable to her, as to any Indian.

Mother Teresa's one souvenir from Las Vegas indicated the unbroken trend of her thinking. Taken by car to the nearby desert so that she could have the peace necessary for the preparation of her talks, she settled herself near a cactus plant to concentrate and contemplate. Before she left the desert, she picked up a few of the long cactus spines which were easily twined into a crown of thorns. This she took back to Calcutta as her only tangible momento of Las Vegas, and it was placed on the head of the crucified Christ hanging behind the altar of her novitiate's stark chapel.

Peoria to Calcutta

The theme of the convention at Las Vegas was "These Works of Love," which was taken from the blessing conferred by Pope John XXIII on every American Catholic woman who participated in the works of mercy for people outside the borders of the United States. His Holiness wrote:

The children, the mothers, the families with whom you share your goods in charity are unknown to you. You will never receive in this life a word of gratitude from them. Yet you spend your precious time on their behalf. But you have the consolation of knowing that *these works of love* performed on behalf of those united to you only by the bond of charity, will last beyond the other good works of your lifetime. These works of love will go with you into eternity, and help you to unite with the source of all love, God.

A part of the lengthy blessing dealt specifically with the Madonna Plan.

This new program which you have entitled 'The Madonna Plan,' besides aiding St. Martha's Clinic in Vatican City, is already spanning the world in support of projects designed to help the mother and child. In areas where motherhood is degraded by poverty, by disease, and by the promulgation of methods of birth prevention that are contrary to the natural law, you, through charity, are emphasizing the sacredness of the function of motherhood: a sacredness symbolized in Our Blessed Lady under whose patronage your efforts are being conducted.

A most telling comment on the working of the Madonna Plan is the story of how it linked Peoria, Illinois, in the heartland of the United States, with Calcutta, India. Beginning in 1958, the Catholic women of the diocese had been collecting funds for the six Mother and Child Clinics founded in Calcutta by Mother Teresa, and after her trip to Las Vegas she wanted to visit Peoria and the surrounding area.

In 1958, Mrs. Robert Hugh Mahoney, then President of the NCCW, was to be the main speaker at the convention of the Diocesan Council of Catholic Women of the Peoria diocese. Because of illness she was unable to speak and suggested that I take her place. I had just returned from India, and filled with what I had seen in Calcutta, I told the story of Mother Teresa and her Missionaries of Charity.

The women of Peoria were struck by the vast abyss which separated their lives from those of the women of Bengal, mothers who also loved their children and wished the best life for them. They felt this gap might be narrowed by charity and, under the leadership of Mrs. Fred Schotthoeffer, Council President, and Mrs. Leon Lamet, National Chairman of the International Relations Committee, they decided to adopt for at least three years, through the Madonna Plan, the mother and child clinics in Calcutta. The adoption would consist not only of collecting money for the clinics, but also of becoming familiar with the land they were in, by studying the history of India, the challenges which met it when it entered freedom, and the problem of the massive refugee influx. Talks and discussions were prepared on various aspects of Indian life, and meetings were scheduled throughout the diocese.

One of the priests of the Peoria diocese, the Reverend William Schumacher, was able to give firsthand details to round out the presentations. He had taken a "mission vacation," spending his holidays observing mission work in Asia. In Calcutta he was introduced to the works of charity of Mother Teresa. From his personal experiences he was able to give more encouragement to the women of Peoria who were establishing a bond of union between themselves and the people of Bengal.

Once a year, a voluntary collection was taken up among the women. Though they could not lessen their contributions to local charities and community needs, these women took on yet another commitment. Through their efforts, thousands of dollars earmarked for Mother Teresa were sent every year to the National Headquarters of NCCW. So when she came to the United States, it seemed only proper that she visit the diocese of Peoria to thank her benefactors. After the artificiality and flamboyancy of Las Vegas, Nevada, Mother Teresa was going to savor the life of Main Street, U.S.A.

The day after we arrived we were taken by car to the town of Henry, a small community in the flat corn belt of Illinois. The visit of Mother Teresa was an important event, and the only place big enough to hold the meeting was the local high school. Buses were chartered from communities all over the diocese to bring families to meet her. Since it was a Sunday the large auditorium was filled to capacity and the audience listened carefully as Father Schumacher introduced Mother Teresa.

She stood up in her rough sari and put her hands together in the traditional Indian greeting as she bowed her head.

"This is the way," she said, "that we greet the people in India."

"I have come from India to thank you and every individual family throughout the States for the kindness and the love you have shown for the work of God which is being done through the Missionaries of Charity. For many years I have been praying with the Sisters that we may be able to do something more for the mother and the child in the slums. As you know, we work only for the poorest of the poor. The amount of things we got was just enough to meet the needs of the day. Now we have three other Sisters who will be soon finished as doctors and will be able to go further in—into the hearts of the slums that up till now we have not been able to go to because of the want of Sisters who could do the work.

"Last year, ending December 31, we had treated 74,000 people that passed through our six dispensaries, that have been cared for and helped. It is your charity that helped keep our work for the mother and child going. But we needed another clinic.

"The whole convent and the children in the slums prayed and it was very strange that in the same week, so to say in the same day, we got the answer. By the morning mail I got a letter from Mrs. Lamet to say that her group had vowed and promised to help the work in India for the mother and the child through your Madonna Plan.

"In the afternoon I had the letter from a lady doctor, an English lady doctor who had seen the work, and she wanted to join the congregation and do the work for the mother and the child. Next day I got a letter to say that the land that I had been looking for, for a seventh clinic, can be ours. So the place, the money, and the persons to do the work came as an answer to a prayer, and today we have seven such clinics where the Sisters, with the lady doctors, Hindu and Mohammedan, work for the same idea, with the same love, with the same devotion for their own people—the people of the slums.

"A high government official said once: 'You and we do the same social work. But the difference between you and us is one that we cannot pass over. You work for somebody and we work for something.' He knew that Somebody is Jesus. But it is Jesus in the disguise of the people suffering in the streets and the slums of our cities.

"I'm sure most of you, through my friend Miss Egan, know how the Congregation of the Missionaries of Charity began. We are now only ten years old, and we have nearly two hundred Sisters. Among them we have a girl from San Diego, one from Germany, one English girl, one from Yugoslavia and myself from Albania. And the rest are all Indian women that come from the best families. That is the beauty of the thing which the Hindu people do not understand—how such girls as these give up their university degrees, give up their home, they give up their social standing, and they come down to help to sanctify those people that are created to the image of God."

She talked of the service given to some of the poorest mothers and children in the world—service that sometimes came too late to save the victims of disease and constant unremitting hunger.

"There was a Hindu mother," she told them, "with two children, little Nirmal and Shunil. One was two years old and the other four. She had walked for several miles to come to the home, but as she was in the last stages of T.B. she collapsed on the way and then the ambulance came to pick

her up. She asked: 'Take me to Mother's home.' Everybody
in Calcutta knows the Mother's home. So they brought her
there and I happened to be in. The mother was gasping. She
took the little hands of her two children, put them in my
hands, and she died. That's all she wanted—to make sure that
the two little ones would be with us."

Mother Teresa finished her talk by referring once more to
the spirit of the Missionaries of Charity and to the spirit of
cooperation which was at work in Calcutta:

"We Missionaries of Charity make a vow of surrendering
ourselves to the poor in this way, we wholly depend on
Divine Providence. When I go around, when I need things, I
don't beg. I have not begged from the time we started to
work, but I go to the people—the Hindus and Moham-
medans, and to the Christians, and I tell them: 'I have come
to give you a chance to do something beautiful for God!'

"More than things and money I need the people themselves to come to the people, to come to the poor, that the
poor may see they are loved. And that is what is happening in
Calcutta!

"We may not have done much work, but we have broken
the wall between the rich and the poor—between the highest
social standing of Brahmin, and the poorest of the poor in the
slums."

After a local boys' choir sang parts of a joyful Mass the
meeting was ended and we went to the school library where a
festive Sunday tea was served.

Mother Teresa and her Sisters never took so much as a
glass of water or a cup of tea offered in hospitality. As they
could not accept it from the poor without depriving them of
the little they had, they would not accept it from anyone,
Mother Teresa explained. While the tea was in progress, she

answered innumerable questions about her work and her congregation. A hastily made cardboard collection box was placed on the tea table—unobtrusively, money was dropped into this box all afternoon, money which totalled a completely unexpected gift of nearly five hundred dollars.

At the end of three years, the women of Peoria decided to continue their link with Calcutta indefinitely. Every year, a large donation is sent through NCCW—Madonna Plan to help support the mother and child clinics in the slums.

After the meeting, Mother Teresa and I were driven to Chicago by a former National Officer of NCCW, Mrs. Walter Scherer. It was a golden October day as we drove through Illinois. Corn fields stretched endlessly on both sides of the road. Every now and then the flat landscape was broken by aluminum bins in which surplus U.S. corn was stored. From storage places such as these the "Food for Peace" program fanned out to famished areas of the earth.

We stopped before a cluster of twenty grain bins and got out of the car. Mother Teresa gazed for a long time at the grain growing and the grain stored from earlier harvests. Her eyes were held by the fields bursting with the richness of yet another bumper crop. "May God bless you," she said, "for what you are doing for our poor, our mothers, our children, our sick and dying, our lepers. I am glad I came here to see this sight and to meet the good people."

Calcutta

One of the clinics helped by these gifts from the women of Peoria was located in the Kidderpore area of Calcutta. Mother Teresa made it a point to visit this once a week. During my stay in Calcutta I accompanied Mother Teresa while she visited the Mother and Child Clinics, travelling always in the mobile clinic our agency had given to the Missionaries of Charity. When we arrived at the Kidderpore Clinic at 8 A.M. the line of patients was already assembled. The clinic consisted of a covered waiting shed, a large ante-room for the dispensing of prescriptions and food, and two examining rooms, one for men and the other for women.

The waiting patients resembled a colony of small tents, for the majority of the women were enveloped in the *burka,* the tent-like garment that fits over the head to protect Muslim women from the public gaze.

When they entered the compound their faces were com-pletely covered with only two round holes of fine net, or a sort of window of loose crocheted work that allowed for see-ing and breathing. Once inside the clinic area, however, the front flap of the *burka* was lifted back or the garment was completely unfastened.

The jewel above the left nostril of even the poorest women shone in the morning sunlight. The younger ones wore long earrings that shook back and forth like bells. Protective coal-blacking outlined the brilliant eyes of even the smallest chil-dren. The cotton *burkas,* in colorful blues, greens, purples, and stark white, gave the patients a look of brilliance, but could hardly conceal the grim and gray lives of these women.

Many were returning for pills, vitamins and drugs given on earlier prescriptions. Among the new cases was a little girl whose eye and cheek had been scalded by hot water, and whose closed, suppurating eyelid made it unlikely that the sight could be saved. There were cases which required hospi-talization, but Mother Teresa explained that it was next to impossible to get some of these women near a hospital. Their lives were lived out in a seclusion made hideous by overcrowding. Yet, as dutiful wives, they only left their court-yards in cases of extreme necessity.

That morning I saw how dreadfully ill a woman often was before she would venture out to get medical help. A rickshaw driver delivered a woman crouching and moaning in agony. When Mother Teresa left her line of patients to study the new arrival she recognized her and hurried to give her an injection. Sitting behind the patient was a rheumy-eyed old woman, fantastically matted and dirty, who tottered out of the rickshaw and began to talk to Mother Teresa. She was the mother of the patient, and took care of her daughter's children.

The younger woman stopped moaning and was carried into the consulting room. Her frail wasted body was enormously distended at the stomach; her stick-like legs were distorted and bloated at the ankles and feet. She was the victim of more than one disease and her heart and kidneys were seriously affected. Mother Teresa gave her further injections, and a supply of medicines and powdered milk was given to the old mother before the two were helped into the rickshaw. The Anglo-Indian woman volunteer at the clinic offered to buy the family a supply of food for the succeeding weeks.

Many of the children examined by the doctor were found to have signs of tuberculosis and were immediately sent to Shishu Bhavan, the children's home, for X-rays. Constant undernourishment, coupled with desperate living conditions which meant sleeping on earthen floors and coping with the damp nights of Calcutta, caused the incidence of lung and throat ailments to soar. A bright and healthy looking little boy joined the line with his mother and baby sister. Mother Teresa asked me to note him especially, and then filled in his story. He had been one of the many chidren afflicted by worms—not tape worms, but what are called in Calcutta red worms. Brought to Shishu Bhavan, he had passed forty worms before his treatment was over. Smaller children in the slums had been known to die of suffocation when the invading worms had so riddled the body that they rose up in the gullet and blocked the throat passage. Worm medicines, adminis-tered with constant care, were effective in banishing the scourge, but the chances of reinvasion were very great.

I could see why Mother Teresa insisted on going herself one morning a week to the Kidderpore dispensary and serv-ing until the last patient had been seen. The security of her presence, even though her services were necessarily limited, gave the women the courage to leave their seclusion and bring their children with them.

Another clinic operated in a room at Shishu Bhavan that had been cut off from the rest of the children's shelter and was reached by a separate entrance. Every Saturday afternoon an Anglo-Indian doctor named Ivy Cecil donated her time to examining and treating needy mothers of the surrounding area.

Dr. Cecil explained to me that the Calcutta Corporation operated four large maternal and child health clinics, offer-ing medical, surgical and obstetrical service to the poor. These clinics, even working overtime, could not meet the needs of the destitute who lived on the fringe of life in the teeming city.

I sat in Dr. Cecil's consulting room one afternoon as the line of patients filed past. They were chiefly follow-up cases who were on the regular treatment rolls, women whose needs became known through the free school and dispensary activi-ties of the Sisters. One thin old woman with a face like an-cient leather presented herself for the first time. I was interested to know her age, because her desiccated, furrowed cheeks and wizened little body brought the word "crone" to my mind. "She won't know how old she is," said Dr. Cecil. "They hardly ever do. But we can work it out."

In reply to the first question, the old lady explained that as for the exact count of years, she could not say. The next question was the age of her oldest child. Her first son, she said, had two children. He had been married about five years, or perhaps more.

"The only way we can estimate the age of the poor," Dr. Cecil explained, "is by getting the approximate ages of children and grandchildren. We count that a girl is about sixteen or seventeen when her first child is born. Her son would probably be between twenty-five and twenty-eight. She is well under fifty, probably about forty-five years old."

This woman was one of many grandmothers and aunts I encountered in Bengal, whose almost sightless eyes, groping walk and discolored loose garments made women of fifty look like hags of ninety. There were the aging widows, many of them widowed since early childhood before the consummation of their marriage, whose shaven skulls erased any distinction between sexes, and seemed to turn them into cadaverous neuters.

No matter what the immediate cause of illness among the poor of Calcutta, it was always complicated by malnutrition—all around the city was the dreadful, unremitting hunger of the poor.

Each family eligible to attend the mother and child clinics received a precious portion of powdered milk—an important factor in the growth or recovery of many of the children. Fresh milk, as sold in Calcutta, was always a health hazard. It was brought down the Hooghly River by milkmen who sold it at stops along the way, and they had almost as much to sell in the city as they had when starting out. City customers were paying for a mixture of milk and water, mostly water from the Hooghly—a river filled with unimaginable filth. Even those who insisted on having the cow milked in front of their doorway could hardly be secure from hazards. City-dwelling cows were covered with the filth of the sidewalks and traffic-filled streets where they so often lay down to rest. City milk-men invented new dodges; many of them wore a rubber tube around the neck, and as the cow was being milked into the customer's bucket, a small stream of water slipped simulta-neously into the same container.

It would be hard for Americans, accustomed to high stan-dards of hygiene, to imagine what this powdered milk, free from impurities, meant to the mothers of ailing children at the dispensaries of the Missionaries of Charity. The effort that resulted in getting the milk to Calcutta was an impres-sive example of intricate planning for human welfare. The sick Indian child was the recipient of a cooperative effort that included the U.S. Government "Food for Peace" program, Catholic Relief Services, the Catholic women of the Peoria diocese, and those vowed to remain by the side of the poor, the Missionaries of Charity.

From such clinics and other social services of the Mission-aries of Charity, came the list of the several hundred families who would receive a regular weekly supply of local foods as part of the Feed-A-Family Program of the National Council of Catholic Women.

The distribution of these food packages, an example of the organizing power of Mother Teresa and her co-workers, took place every Friday afternoon at Shishu Bhavan, the children's home.

One mother who came to the clinic seeking aid was enrolled in the NCCW plan of regular help. She had three small children with her and told Mother Teresa her husband had just died of tuberculosis. Now she had to go out and get a job.

As with so many of these women, a job meant just one thing, washing the dishes for families in the center of Calcutta, many of whom numbered sons, daughters and all grandchildren, families with an enormous dishwashing task. The woman was slight and tired looking, and she told Mother that she might get a similar job in two or three families so that she could at least continue to pay the rent. She could expect to earn three rupees a month from each family (about seventy-five cents in American money) for this work, in addition to her own food and possibly some rice to take home to her children.

The woman, Apurna Shaha, wanted the Sisters to take her children at Shishu Bhavan during the day, until she found work. Afterwards, her eldest son Amal could take care of them at home. Amal, thin and undersized, was a small boy of ten whose brilliant eyes followed every word of the conversation. Another child was sick and had been left with a neighbor. Mother Teresa, who knew the case, explained later that the middle child was tubercular. She agreed to take the three children for a short period until Apurna Shaha had found some work, and it was decided then that this mother was to be enrolled in the Feed-A-Family program. She was given a green folded card indicating this, and I filled it out in the name of the NCCW.

The next Friday she appeared to pick up Amal and the other children, and stood in line to get her seven pounds of rice and other basic foods. She was on a line that included the mothers of two hundred of the most abject families in Calcutta. The majority of the women who came that afternoon had been dispossessed from their home towns and villages. Most of them were widows, but a number had ill or unemployed husbands. One by one the women took their seven pounds of food in containers that they had brought with them. Some of the very poorest carried the grains in the tied-up ends of their saris.

A number of them knew English and I was surprised when I found that among the refugees from Pakistan were a few names like Teresa Gomes, Maria da Cruz and Cecilia Rozario. These were all from "Dacca side," as the saying goes, and their families had borne Portuguese names for generations, having come under the care of Portuguese priests, in the ancient Padroado of the East of the Portuguese Church. Other names, such as Arikmary Samuel, indicated Tamil origin, and belonged to the migrants from South India.

In a normal American family seven pounds of food would mean very little. But this amount, given out regularly every Friday, meant a weekend without excessive hunger for the destitute of Calcutta. Twenty-eight pounds of food a month, received without fail over a long period of time, allowed these families to maintain their unity and to save their few rupees for the other basic necessities of living.

When I was in Calcutta, 250 green NCCW cards had been distributed, each card representing one of the city's most destitute families, and representing also a way to help meet and surmount the threat of family dissolution. Many families assailed by hunger and homelessness succumbed to the enveloping misery, the boys taking to full-time begging, the girls from twelve onward to outright prostitution or to enforced seclusion, serving in households where in return for their keep they were used as domestic slaves and as "second wives."

The decision to give out the foods on a weekly basis was arrived at because few such families had any way of storing things. The families who had even enough room to lie down at night were considered lucky. These refugees needed every ounce of initiative to survive the long years ahead, and a small, regular food supplement was the most practical way to keep this initiative alive. In special cases, the family received a small grant of funds for rent or clothing from the NCCW donations. Each received the equivalent of only twenty dollars a year, but the significance of the gift was hardly measurable.

To over seven thousand families a food package was given out monthly. I saw the line at Shishu Bhavan expeditiously handled by Sister Benedicta, in charge of relief projects, and a corps of women volunteers.

Every morning of the week, a group from a different *bustee* was supplied with the U.S. surplus food available. Sometimes a five pound bag of wheat flour, sometimes cornmeal, and always powdered milk. When there had been surplus butter in the form of butter oil, the poor of Calcutta, so often prey to tuberculosis and various deficiency diseases, responded as though receiving manna from heaven. Ghee, the local clarified butter, was beyond the pocket of all but the well-to-do. But whatever items were available from the mountains of surplus produced in the U.S. were received with wonder and gratitude by the needy of Calcutta.

New York City

Before beginning her return trip to India, Mother Teresa flew with me to New York City. As we arrived at the airport late at night, we could not go to the convent where she was to be a guest. We put up instead at the Leo House, a plain hospice founded originally for Catholic immigrants. With its chapel and quiet, private dining room, it was a natural stopping off place for members of religious orders in transit through the city.

Mother Teresa had often mentioned to me her gratitude to an American, Mother Anna Dengel, and to the Medical Mission Sisters of Philadelphia. Shortly after she had obtained permission to leave a strictly confined teaching order in Calcutta, she had been invited to live with the Medical Mission Sisters at Patna, some two hundred miles away.

At their Patna Holy Family Hospital, the Sisters brought to Indian women their skills as nurses, laboratory experts and doctors. In her months as their guest, Mother Teresa received a course in practical nursing, a brief, immensely valuable experience for a woman who was to take on the burdens of the destitute and dying in a refugee-swollen city.

When she prepared to leave Patna, Mother Teresa was already enveloped in the cotton sari of India. The American Sisters as their parting gift gave her a sturdy pair of sandals. These came to be known as the "Patna sandals," since they were passed on to other members of the Missionaries of Charity.

By the time Mother Teresa made her first visit to the United States, the Medical Mission Sisters had become a Congregation, and the Motherhouse, now called a Generalate, had been moved to Rome. Mother Dengel, foundress and Mother General, was stationed in Rome to unify and expand an order that took its work of healing into four continents.

The morning after our arrival in the Leo House, we went to the chapel for an early Mass. A woman in the grey habit of the Medical Mission Sisters was in the pew directly in front of

us. As we turned to leave after the Mass, she also got up.
Then I recognized her as Mother Dengel. After I had presented to each other two Twentieth-Century Mother Foundresses, Mother Dengel explained that she had just flown in
from Rome to take part in a meeting in New York City. We
discovered later that she had been named "Woman of the
Year" by a non-sectarian federation of women's organizations.

We went together to breakfast in the Leo House dining-
room where Mother Teresa was finally able to express personally her thanks for the hospitality and training she had
received from Mother Dengel's Order. Mother Dengel had
heard much about the work of Mother Teresa and the Missionaries of Charity. She wanted to know what the young
Indian sisters were doing in Calcutta, where they would be
working next, and what courses of study they would be following. In turn, she answered Mother Teresa's questions
about the hospitals and clinics of the Medical Mission Sisters
in Pakistan, India, the United States, Africa and Latin
America. There was a deep mutual respect between the two
women; there was a complete dedication about them and
about their interest in each other's mission to mankind.

In appearance they presented some contrast. Mother Teresa, short and vibrant, was just approaching middle age. One
might say she was poet of the poor and lowly, after the manner of St. Francis. She shared in their daily lot and served as
their voice before the affluent classes of the world. She was
not a specialist, but a woman who found new and creative
ways to express woman's great gift of compassion in the up-
heavals of the twentieth century. If she could do no more,
she would trundle a dying man in a wheelbarrow from his

gutter resting place to a shelter where he could die a human death.

Mother Dengel was a woman who had put the highest of skills at the service of the lowliest and most obscure of suffering humankind. No less compassionate, she had found another way to reach those in need—especially Muslim women in purdah whose husbands would not allow them to be cared for by a male doctor, and women who had been treated as chattels, as mere things, from time immemorial. Even her quiet grey uniform and practical white-banded, black head-dress spoke clearly of her eminently practical mission of scientific skill. Mother Dengel was already past middle age, ample and still vigorous, with a rich voice and a slight trace of accent from her native Austrian Tyrol.

As they talked, I thought of some strange similarities that had marked their careers. Both had been moved to lives of special and even revolutionary service by the needs of India, Mother Dengel by the unmet health needs of the women, Mother Teresa by the anguish and homelessness that grew to a dread climax in the 1940's, the era of Partition. Oddly enough, though they both came from South Europe, they had launched their careers in Ireland. Mother Dengel, who in 1913 was given a scholarship at Cork University through the Scottish medical missionary, Dr. Agnes McLaren, remained in Ireland until 1920, when she left for India to direct the St. Catherine's Hospital for Women and Children founded by Dr. McLaren. Mother Teresa had been admitted to the Institute of the Blessed Virgin in Dublin in 1924. Later that year, she sailed for Calcutta and never left the country of her adoption until she flew to the meeting in Las Vegas.

But of the essence of their similarity was their common championship of the most despised of the earth, their disdain for the privilege and might of the world. A deeper essential yet, it seemed to me, was their identity with that strong, most revolutionary woman who called out in the prayer we call the *Magnificat:* "He has shown might in his arm, he has scattered the proud in the conceit of their hearts. He has put down the mighty from their seats, and has exalted the lowly. He has filled the hungry with good things, and the rich he has sent empty away."

4

Madonna Plan spans the globe

THE founding of a new program under the Foreign Relief Committee had been under consideration for a time, but the immediate spark was a request from Monsignor Andrew P. Landi, who reminded us of the St. Martha Clinic inside the walls of Vatican City. For thirty years this clinic had served the mothers from the poorest and most crowded sections of Rome. Besides medical care, the infants needed a fortified milk formula to build up their strength against the health hazards of the poor in any city, but especially in a city as old and full of antiquated dwellings as Rome.

The milk formula favored by the volunteer doctor was an American product and Monsignor Landi wondered if American Catholic women would make a yearly supply available to this unique Vatican charity. Putting this new program under Our Lady's special protection, Miss Margaret Mealey christened it The Madonna Plan, and in our first appeal we explained the reason for the name.

"What is the Madonna Plan? This is the question that you will ask, and that surely will be asked of you. The Madonna, to us Catholic women, is symbolic of the sacred function of motherhood, of its cooperation with God in the formation of a human body to house an immortal soul.

"Of great concern is the growing view that motherhood is solely a biological function without social or even moral aspects. A news magazine recently published the shocking news that in crowded Puerto Rico one fifth of the women between the ages of 15 and 40 had been sterilized. Sterilization, birth control and abortion are presented as answers to problems ranging from family financial difficulties to the halting of overpopulation.

"Mother and child clinics, maternity hospitals, training centers in Christian homemaking, staffed by dedicated religious sisters and lay women, operate in hardpressed areas of the globe. Through Catholic Relief Services—N.C.W.C., your gift can reach the Dispensary of St. Martha in Vatican City, the Clinics of Mother Teresa in Calcutta, and even the far off Ryukyu Islands where American Dominican Missionaries are training young girls in child care.

"In the name of Mary, a poor woman who knew exile and the heart-piercing sword of sorrow, make your gift now for the mother and child of today, victims of not only exile and hunger, but of those doctrines that seek out the child to destroy him."

The Madonna Plan was founded at a time when "the Question" of spending aid funds on information regarding artificial methods for the prevention of conception was a presence in the halls and meeting rooms of the United Nations in New York City. It presented a positive program designed to arouse consciences to the undeniable needs and alarming situations that moved leaders to call for population control. Its small projects showed a development along many of the same lines as the Maternity and Child Health Centers of the United Nations Childrens Fund, most often referred to as UNICEF. The excellent technical assistance and training programs of UNICEF were a natural growth from straight relief, from the "cup of milk" approach, just as Madonna Plan, on the voluntary level, grew out of feeding and relief efforts.

While "the Question" was haunting many international aid and planning debates, Madonna Plan was indicating how voluntary programs could bring real help to the mother and child. It showed the enormous work being carried out by religious sisters and volunteers in thousands of clinics, maternity hospitals and training centers in Asia, Africa and Latin America. Under the Madonna Plan, needed additions could be made to existing programs formulated by local groups overseas, often women's groups.

Rome

The Madonna Plan's first allocation in 1958, a year's supply of Dryco milk formula for the St. Martha's Clinic, Vatican City, was so efficacious that it was requested and supplied for years to come.

On my next visit to Rome, Monsignor Landi arranged for me to visit the clinic which had been the first to receive Madonna Plan help. I went through the St. Martha Gate, to the left of St. Peter's Basilica. This is one of the gates of entry to Vatican City, and as it is a sovereign state, we were stopped by a Swiss Guard. Anyone not recognized by the Guardsmen on duty had to identify himself and his destination.

But the poorest mothers of Rome came and went freely through the gate, carrying their babies in their arms. They were regular visitors, and the Guards knew them and waved them on with a smile. In all the pictures of visitors and dignitaries entering Vatican City, I had never seen a photograph of Rome's poor mothers, who have been coming through the St. Martha Gate on two clinic days every week for over thirty years.

The clinic room was large, square and airy, brighter than other rooms in the Vatican because of its plain white walls and shining white tiles, and its large hospital-type ceiling lamps. Fifty mothers from the misery-scourged slums of Rome were present for the regular weekly check-up. Some had brought their babies from the *borgata* of Prima Valle, a working class quarter at a distance from the center of Rome. The *borgate,* or poorer sections of Rome, are situated at the end of extended bus rides so tourists seldom come in contact with the dramatic poverty of Rome. Even the newest housing that I saw in Prima Valle had no central heating, and the flimsy construction was poor protection against the damp and cold of the Roman winter. One or two rooms to a family— eight or ten members in a family—was the rule. Inadequate as they were, they were better than the older slums. At least on sunny days children could escape to the open spaces that surrounded the dwellings.

Others had come from the nearby *"Quartiere del Papa,"* the Papal Quarter, where, on narrow enclosed streets, they lived in buildings that were three or four hundred years old. These heavy grey stone edifices were once the cavernous haunts of the Roman nobility and the members of the Papal court. Then the Papal Quarter had been the hub of Roman social and diplomatic life. But what had sufficed for a single household in the sixteenth and seventeenth centuries, had to accommodate hundreds of families in the twentieth. I had seen how a family of seven, mother, father and five children, ate, slept, played and studied in one damp stonewalled room in an ancient structure on Via Gonfalone. There was only one window, and the damp stale air was hardly ever freshened. The only way to stay warm was to conserve body heat with layers of clothing.

At the end of the clinic day, a squat woman with a strong, lined face and grizzled gray hair came in carrying a plump, smiling baby boy I thought must be her grandson. But this was her own son she explained, and she was forty-six years old. Her brown eyes softened and she smiled as she looked at him. "This is my Angelo. He is a gift of God to me and my husband. Sister helps us to keep him strong."

Korea

The Thirty-Eighth Parallel separating North and South Korea might seem a far cry from Vatican City. Yet a direct line united the St. Martha Clinic with the St. Columban Clinic located smack on the Thirty-Eighth Parallel at the edge of the buffer zone, or No Man's Land that serves as barrier. A half dozen Columban Sisters, nurses, laboratory technicians, and a doctor, opened their clinic in 1957 at Chunchon on the very border of the Free World. After the Madonna Plan was inaugurated with the help to St. Martha's Clinic, a grant went to St. Columban's, which stood almost in the shadow of "Honest John," the great missile-launching rocket.

Sister Enda, the young Irish clinic doctor, visited our New York office on her return trip to Korea from Ireland. Her descriptions, and the accounts of Miss Sighle Kennedy, the Project Supervisor for Korea, provided firsthand details.

When the Columban Sisters, all from Ireland, moved from their first Korean project, a hospital in Mokpo, in Southwest Korea, they chose Chunchon because there was no scientific medicine in the area. The province, known as Kang Won Do, counted a million inhabitants in a largely mountainous area. The steep Diamond Mountains long formed an effective barrier to communication and to contact with more advanced ideas.

Medicine there was, but a medicine composed of a wild and dangerous amalgam of Chinese traditions, half-understood western medical concepts and village witchcraft. In the very isolated villages, the only medical resource was the local witch, who practiced her healing arts to the accompaniment of wild whirling and lamentations. Men who had picked up the rudiments of western medical arts set themselves up as full-fledged doctors, and were known to perform dangerous and useless surgery on sick and injured villagers.

One would think that a clinic giving the best of medical care by doctors and nurses trained in the finest of modern hospitals would be swamped by patients as soon as word got around of its presence. But this was not the case. The Sisters at the clinic had to meet a tremendous challenge in gaining the confidence of the isolated people and in training them to a new outlook. The Koreans were understandably attached to the traditional healing practices that were a part of their cultural pattern. There were times when the Sisters lost patients to the local medical man or the village witch.

But before long, those who made the trek over mountain paths to Chunchon began to show the effects of scientific healing and of the extra foods and vitamins issued to the undernourished. The list of patients slowly grew longer.

Sister Mary Enda wrote us:

"I could write a book about the Clinic—but there is barely time to breathe. We start work at 7:30 a.m. each day, but the people are waiting outside the gate from 4:00 a.m.—mothers with starved and dying babies, and they themselves so thin and gaunt. It is not hard to guess that many a time they have to 'skip-a-meal' through sheer poverty. Men and women on the line are often near the end of the road from tuberculosis and cancer. There are cases of leprosy and snake-bite, and every kind of skin disease—and a thousand things besides. All are patiently waiting for the nurse to open the doors and let them in. Then they have to take their place in the line for three or four hours till their turn comes. The only ones who get preference are the very, very sick. We have an average of about four hundred patients at the Clinic every day—some days there are over five hundred."

The Sisters began to make emergency calls by jeep when the requests came in. Around the province of Kang Won Do were stationed thirty Columban priests. People who became ill ran to the priest in their distress. They often would be driven off in the priest's jeep for first aid at St. Columban's.

The reference to "skip-a-meal" in Sister Mary Enda's letter was a reminder of a way to raise money for the Madonna Plan. During Lent, the Catholic women of the United States were asked to "Skip-A-Meal," and give what they had saved to Madonna Plan-NCCW. In adopting this scheme, they were following the example of Austrian Catholic women, who had on a national scale missed one meal a day in order to help hungry and homeless Koreans. For Korean mothers, Sister Mary Enda's patients, the skipping of a meal was a regular, involuntary happening. In fact, the province of Kang Won Do was so poor that one bad harvest could bring thousands to the point of real starvation. In the mountains whipped by the bone-chilling winds from the north, hunger was an enforced and constant companion.

When Mrs. Ulric Scott, the Foreign Relief Chairman of

NCCW, saw the pictures of St. Columban's Clinic, she decided to take them back to the women in her diocese, St. Paul, Minnesota. The women of St. Paul decided that they would vary the method of collecting funds, substituting for the "Skip-A-Meal" a new method known as the "Vanishing Luncheon." Mrs. Scott explained that the "Vanishing Luncheon" scheme had definite advantages in that it brought the women together to discuss overseas needs and gave them a chance to learn some of the splendid efforts that were being carried on in remote areas of the world.

Mrs. Scott told the women of her diocese the facts about St. Columban's Clinic. Then she suggested: "Would you volunteer to have a party of ten to luncheon? As hostess you supply the luncheon—or it could be a tea or just a coffee meeting. Take time to discuss the project. Here is a letter from Mother Calasanctius, Director of St. Columban's Clinic, that tells you about the needs and the challenges of work on the 38th Parallel in Korea.

"Collect a dollar from each of the ten women, and a pledge that each will have a party of five. Collect a dollar from each of the party of five, and turn the proceeds over to the original hostess of ten. Thus the luncheon party vanishes and there is $60.00 to help these Sisters fulfill their great mission at the front line of the Free World."

All over the St. Paul Archdiocese the "Vanishing Luncheon" scheme took hold. Some women started off with a party of twenty, and each of the twenty entertained ten, and so on down to five. So successful was the unusual idea that St. Columban's received two hundred dollars every month for years on end.

Mother Calasanctius wrote:

"It is a wonderful thing that a Vanishing Luncheon

project of Catholic women can help bring western medicine to a Korean mountain province on the other side of the world. The twenty-four hundred dollars for this year will allow us to count on a steady stream of much-needed special medicines. Your gifts are God-sent indeed."

While Mother Calasanctius went quietly about her tasks of provisioning and recording for the Clinic, and Sister Mary Enda performed prodigies of medical care, the air would be rent by the dud missiles launched by Honest John that exploded, as a newsman said, "like scalded cats," in the air above the "No-Man's-Land" of the Parallel.

Karachi

The Madonna Plan grant to the Lemmens Center in Karachi takes on meaning against the background of the recent history of that seaport city. I flew into Karachi in 1955, a few years after it became the capital of Pakistan.

This city, Karachi, was once known as the cleanest in Asia, at a time when its population was no more than a quarter of a million. After the Indian sub-continent was partitioned into India and Pakistan, several million people were displaced from their homes and a great stream of the dispossessed converged on Karachi. No one knows how many, but at least a million came in from the hinterland, especially from the area of the Punjab where Moslem proprietors left their homes and possessions and went into Pakistan. Among the landless workers who were displaced were a goodly number of Christians who had belonged to the lower Hindu caste, the caste which supplied the sweepers and other menial workers having to do with sanitation.

In Karachi they joined a great army of street sweepers. At dawn with their little brooms they would go out along

Karachi's broad downtown streets and clean away the refuse left by the day's passage of people, camel carts and the horse-driven *tonga* carts. The army of sweepers, Moslem and Christian, did their best for the over-crowded city. But there was little they could do for themselves.

At night the poorest of the sweepers spread a piece of cloth on the sidewalk as their bed. Often the curbstone was their pillow. So fierce was the fight for a place to sleep, that when a man was placed on trial in Karachi for killing a fellow worker, the defense's plea was that the victim had appropriated the sidewalk sleeping area which the first worker had long considered his own. The more fortunate of the sweepers found one-room, stone-floored, and stonewalled houses in a poor section known as the "Slaughterhouse." Here amid the smells surrounding animal slaughter and waste, they tried to maintain some family unity and personal dignity.

During my stay in Karachi I was taken to meet one of the leaders of the Slaughterhouse community. His one room house had a table and a single chair. The fact that he was Christian was clear from the gaudy lithograph of the Sacred Heart which hung on the wall. On the shelf were some brightly colored plates and a few cups, probably the only eating utensils the family owned. I sat down on the chair and talked to the family through an interpreter. The father was a very erect Punjabi land worker with flashing eyes and a mustache which must have been copied from that of a British officer of the old colonial days.

Came the question, "Will the lady take some tea?"

I explained I was in a hurry and wanted to meet some other families, and got up to leave. I was detained before the door of the little home to watch the near-naked children playing in the dust and filth. When I entered the next house, there was the usual religious picture in vivid colors. There was no furniture at all, except for one chair. I sat down on it and we had a little chat. Then I was invited into the third house in the row.

There was always, however, a delay in going from one home to another. I realized that this deliberate halt gave the men just enough time to transfer the one wooden chair from house to house so that the visitor would have a place to sit.

In the midst of stench and pervading dust, these displaced people had somehow retained the dignity of their lives. Their homes were swept clean and they never neglected to offer the visitor a cup of tea. No one could be poorer than the families that I visited at the Slaughterhouse. They were all sweepers, the lowest job in the scale. They were all refugees and close to destitution; in addition some of them were a Christian minority in a Moslem land.

Each story was about the same. They had been landless agricultural workers from the Punjab and had lost their work in the chaos that occurred after the former landowners had left their holdings and before the new landlords had taken over. In all I was asked to visit about eight homes.

Shortly after my visit to the Slaughterhouse we received a request from a group of volunteers who had set up a welfare and medical center for the people of that area.

One of the activities of this center, which was called the Lemmens Center in honor of the Dutch monsignor and welfare leader, was to cooperate in "The Cleaner Karachi Week." Inundated as it was by the refugees, Karachi had fallen far from being "the cleanest city of Asia" but many efforts were made to return it to something of its former status. The program opened with a parade of school children carrying banners and shouting slogans. Tasks were given to the children every morning in the classroom. A lecture was given in Urdu to a rally of about two thousand people in the Slaughterhouse area on sanitation, the diseases caused by flies, and the need for personal cleanliness.

The lecture was made more interesting by songs with the accompaniment of a harmonium. Talks on cleanliness were even given to groups of waiting patients at the Lemmens Center Clinic. During the week a large garbage can was presented by the municipal community to the Slaughterhouse area. Members of the Lemmens Center, together with volunteers from the area, operated a spraying machine over the whole section, as part of the anti-fly campaign. A group of teen-age boys were given badges and sent to clean the area and to check on hawkers and some petty shopkeepers. They collected the garbage in baskets and emptied the garbage in the municipal garbage can.

As a result of "The Cleaner Karachi Week" a committee of Slaughterhouse leaders, including some women, was formed to work out further health programs for the area. In this way women could get together and discuss such matters as cleanliness in the home, the cleaning out of blocked house drains, cleanliness of person and for their children.

Participation in the "Cleaner Karachi Week" was only one of the activities of the Lemmens Center, but it illustrates how a welfare center founded and directed by volunteers can play a significant part in community betterment projects. The medical services of the center were of great importance to the whole surrounding area.

A Pakistani woman, Dr. Monica Smith, President of the Lemmens Center, gave regular medical service at the clinic, on Tuesdays for pre-natal cases and on Fridays for general patients. Because of this service she was able to reach the families with food and other help, and inaugurated home visits for the chronically ill.

Other activities initiated by the Lemmens Center included a very popular sewing class and a midwife's training project. Most of the babies in Pakistan are delivered by midwives called *dhais,* who have absorbed superstitions as well as the knowledge of the ages, and have little or no knowledge of the need of cleanliness and hygiene. One course was given especially for the midwives who operated in the Slaughterhouse area, by the matron in a maternity hospital and a registered nurse. Fourteen *dhais* completed the course and attended practical demonstrations in a maternity home and in the Holy Family Hospital conducted by the Medical Mission Sisters. To their new-found knowledge the *dhais* could add a practical midwifery kit supplied by UNICEF, and the advice of trained people at the Lemmens Center. Madonna Plan grants helped these efforts for several years.

Egypt

"We call them 'The Sitting Ones,' " said Gail Malley. "When we ask them what they are doing, they invariably answer, 'We are sitting at home.' Until the age of eleven or twelve, there is still something joyous and quick in the face and gestures of a young girl. Then suddenly life changes. She must sit indoors. When she does go out, it is behind the veil. There is no question of more development as a person."

Gail had just returned from Egypt. She was talking, not only about women living according to the Muslim code, but also about those in the Coptic villages of Upper Egypt. The Coptic Christians, some of them united with the Holy See, lived in a region where ruined and abandoned monasteries recalled the great days of the first Desert Fathers.

She was one of the Grail girls who penetrate the most exotic environments to help people realize in their lives that they are children of God. She had come to know and love Egypt during the four years she had served as secretary to the Reverend Henry Ayrout, S.J., the Director of the Catholic Association for Free Schools in Upper Egypt. A linguist, she had mastered Arabic with the same speed that she had Dutch, Spanish, and French. She showed us some pictures of gay little girls, of older girls carrying water from the well, and of a mother and child in their little home. They seemed to us to bear a strong resemblance to the way artists picture Nazareth. Irene Dalgiewicz, the Catholic Relief Services Project Supervisor for Africa, and I studied the lovely pensive faces of the women of this too little-known Christian community.

Gail explained: "The black veil is an indication of the shadow that falls over their lives. At the age when they would be eager to learn about life and make a contribution to their village, they are shut up behind the walls. And they remain the 'Sitting Ones' until they are given in marriage. They can of course go out for a few important occasions. The Christian girls can attend church or a religious meeting. But the *melaya,* the black veil, falls over them from head to foot before they leave their home enclosure."

Catholic Relief Services already had a large welfare program in conjunction with Egyptian governmental agencies. Egypt's Ministry of Health had inaugurated a heroic medical expansion plan in an effort to reach the ailing amongst the poorest townspeople and villagers. Increased medical care was not effective without increased food. Our agency brought in supplementary food—corn meal, wheat, powdered milk and other foods for nearly seven hundred thousand persons on the rolls of the Health Ministry's network of hospitals and dispensaries.

Gail told us of the Grail's plan to open a welfare center in Akhmim and this seemed to be a natural target for Madonna Plan aid. This aid began in August 1960 with the inauguration of the center. We set aside two hundred dollars monthly for the first three years' work. In giving aid, the Madonna Plan of NCCW could not initiate new projects, nor bear all the costs of a new clinic, dispensary or training center. But it could, as in this case, strengthen the hands of those who were opening up new avenues of service for the mother and child. The Akhmim project was the first Madonna Plan effort in Egypt. The land of Egypt, of course, has a special attraction for Christians since it is the one soil outside the Holy Land on which we know that Christ trod. There is a place called Mary's Well, where, by tradition, the Holy Family stopped for refreshment on their flight from Herod. In the desert of the Thebaid in the Nile Valley, the Egyptian Christians were the first hermits and started the first monasteries of the Christian world.

Akhmim is on the left bank of the Nile, about equidistant from Cairo to the north and Mount Sinai to the northwest across the bay of Suez. There the Commandments of God were handed to Moses written on the tables of the law. The Commandments of God were so dear to the people of Akhmim that in the days of Diocletian, 8140 of them were martyrs for the faith on Christmas night in the year 284. The Street of the Martyrs commemorates the pouring out of their blood on that far Christmas. Now, the bells of the Christian churches are still heard along with the call of the muezzin from the minarets in a city which is one-third Christian.

It was to this city, one of the oldest inhabited places on the face of the earth, that the Grail team came. Akhmim was the fifth city to be built on a site continuously inhabited by man for over five thousand years. It still has visible reminders of former presences, of the Pharaohs, of the Byzantines, and of the Christians who witnessed to their faith in blood. The narrow streets of Akhmim are uneven because of the ruined remains of other immemorial streets underneath.

Just before Christmas 1960, Gail wrote me that she was really at home in Akhmim, in the house on the Street of Martyrs that Father Ayrout had made available to the Grail girls. "We are every day more grateful," she told us, "for the chance to work in the heart of Upper Egypt, in a town that still has and lives from its traditions.

"The days and weeks begin to have their rhythm. The program is finding a shape. In the mornings, we have the kindergarten.

"At about seven-thirty each morning the first knock comes at the door, and there, a little higher than the doorstep, stands one or another of our fifty children—a large handkerchief proudly pinned to the brightly colored dress or tunic, a cloth sack containing a midmorning snack tightly held and immediately described: 'I've got a sweet potato today, Big Sister,' then relinquished with supreme confidence. The children are three, four and five years old, Christian and Moslem, from families fairly representative of Akhmim's population; weavers, a grocer, cloth merchants, coppersmiths, tinsmiths, ironers, carpenters, an Orthodox priest, are among the fathers of our children."

With the help of a local doctor, the children were given needed medical help, especially in the matter of eye cleansing and eye drops. Parents began to send bottles for eye drops for the whole family. The contacts with the families resulted in visits and in informal discussions where such topics as cleanliness, hygiene and feeding for babies, covering food to protect it from flies, and many other concrete matters of daily living were taken up by the girls and women.

A few months later we received the good news that "The Sitting Ones," who were put to hibernate in the enclosure of the home when the first signs of womanhood appeared, were allowed to take part in the activities of the welfare center. "Their parents permit them to attend religious activities, and we fall conveniently—though a bit unconventionally—into this category." Another activity for these girls was an Arts and Crafts course. Already some of the first products of the course, table mats and baskets, were sold through contacts in Cairo. The girls in charge of the Center hoped that this course would be the beginning of home industry on the part of the girls—useful home industry was a program much encouraged by the Egyptian Government.

Two other groups of teen-age girls used the facilities of the Center. Some of the girls were in Eadadi, the junior high school. Responding to the beginnings of emancipation, they studied very hard. They came to ask the Grail girls for help with their lessons, particularly French and English. They used the small library at the Center, spending hours poring over magazines and books that they would never see otherwise. But sometimes studies were interrupted by a rhythm of life that was common to Europe in earlier ages. When a convenient opportunity appeared, the girl was plucked from her accustomed life and given in marriage. A girl of thirteen, just finishing her first year of Eadadi, and first in all the subjects in her class, was married to a forty-five year old man. His mother, who had kept house for him, could no longer manage the housework alone, and so he arranged for a wife with the parents of this girl.

A third group consisted of girls who had had the responsibility of a younger brother and sister from the time they themselves were six or seven years old. The picture of the "little mother," carrying a younger child on her hip, or leading a littler one by the hand, is a familiar one in Africa and Asia. These girls, who were to be married anyway, were never sent to the Egyptian schools, which provided free education. Their brothers, however, all learned to read and write in the public education system because literacy would help them get higher pay. A course in reading and writing was planned for illiterate girls.

But all of the groups of girls were interested in one course—sewing. The first activity of the Center, as originally planned, had been a small dispensary, staffed by an Egyptian nurse-midwife. She was prevented from coming, and there could therefore be no dispensary service.

"It was a disappointment," wrote Gail, "but we have realized that there is perhaps something providential in this. From our contacts with various other centers we have learned that small teams beginning with a dispensary and other directly medical work, have a tendency to be overwhelmed by it. Fortunately the government has already attacked medical problems on a nation-wide scale, setting up hospitals and clinics all over the country. In Akhmim there is a hospital."

Instead, the Grail girls were better able to listen to the interests expressed by the women and girls. They were besieged with demands to start a sewing class. This seemed a secondary matter in contrast to courses in hygiene and sanitation, and their first reply was an automatic "Later." But as the courses in the seemingly more basic field of health did not materialize, more attention was finally paid to the incessant call for sewing classes.

"We only appreciated the value of this enthusiasm as we came gradually deeper into the homes and realized what a rare thing such a sign of life is. Then we saw with sudden clarity that this was the 'felt need' with which we must begin, no matter how urgent other needs must be.

"We even began to see the logic of their argumentation: 'I keep my house as my mother and her mother before her kept it; I have my babies as women have always had them—it's good enough for me. But my neighbor has a sewing machine. She makes all her own and her children's clothes on it, and earns some money on the side sewing other peoples' clothes. *That* would change my life!' "

For those in passage through Egypt, who saw the women of working families swathed in their black all-enveloping *melayas,* it would seem as though their clothing ran to the somber. But once home they throw off the shroud-like veiling, and revel in dresses of the brightest colors. Clothes were their chief possession and one of their most important preoccupations. An important part of their dowry at marriage was a supply of clothing. One girl, whose father was a poor weaver, brought as her dowry thirty colorful dresses, and nothing more. For these she had worked as a servant in a family for a whole year, earning sixty piasters, less than two dollars a month. The sewing course was the focus on which the various groups of girls and women, literate and illiterate, emancipated or "sitting ones," married or unmarried, were united. So large was the number of students, and so enthusiastic the desire to learn the actual use of the sewing machine, that the class had to be divided into two groups—one of young girls, the other of married women. The division worked out successfully, since the girls were mostly interested in putting the first stitches on their trousseaux, while the mothers were concerned with making clothes for their children.

"We have begun," Gail told me in a chatty letter, "with the sewing of underwear. This permits us to concentrate for a moment on the sewing rather than on style or pattern. The women bring their old dresses, which are taken apart, mended, then used for underwear and children's clothes. This has an important educative value, because mending is practically an unknown art, except for occasionally sewing together two sides of a large rent."

Even in such simple affirmations of interest as a desire for a sewing class and sewing machines, the women were asserting the fact that they were persons. The fact that their "felt need" met an assent was important in a setting where women hardly counted. A father or mother, when asked the number of children they had, would give the number of boys only. A woman was not referred to by her name, but by the name of her son, for example as Mahmoud's mother.

Gail wrote: "Every visit is at the same time a revelation of the depth and resilience of human nature. We find dignity, generosity, patience, hospitality, joy—and so many other qualities that fill us with humility and thankfulness.

"We feel more and more strongly that it is in the field of helping woman to discover her dignity and personality that we have a contribution to make—using of course very concrete methods, care of house and children, cooking, sewing, and hygiene, but never losing sight of the fact that we are dealing with persons, whose need to be human is the deepest unexpressed demand."

Uganda

Just forty miles north of the line of the equator in Uganda, the venturesome Grail women set up one of their most fascinating projects. It was the Grail Training Center, located in the town of Mubende, equidistant from Lake Victoria to the east, Lake Albert to the west. Even here the great

Nile River plays a part, since the East Nile flows into Lake Albert, and the Victoria Nile meanders through rich equatorial land into the great lake.

In 1960, help converged on the Center from Catholic women's organizations in Canada, New Zealand, Australia, West Germany, Italy, Spain, and from the United States through the Madonna Plan of NCCW. The genesis of this international help bears telling. The Training Center was the Community Development training school for the Catholic Women's Clubs of Uganda. This program was dovetailed with a government program of the Uganda Government. Also participating with the government were groups affiliated with the Salvation Army, the World Young Women's Christian Association, and the Commission of the Churches on International Affairs. For all of these, the Uganda Government requested help from UNICEF in the form of training equipment, cooking and sewing equipment, and all sorts of transport, including bicycles, motorcycles and Land Rovers.

The UNICEF office at the United Nations Headquarters in New York informed the representatives of the various organizations of the request of the Uganda Government, indicating that its help in equipment would be limited and suggesting that the international organizations of the Uganda groups might want to extend help. Miss Alba Zizzamia, at that time UN representative of the World Union of Catholic Women's Organizations, received the referral. Miss Zizzamia had travelled extensively in Africa, and had visited Uganda. She analyzed and interpreted the requests from the Catholic Women's Clubs and forwarded them to the headquarters of the World Union of Catholic Women's Leagues in Paris. She also communicated with the National Council of Catholic Women. WUCWO in turn sent out the appeal and the Catholic women of seven countries joined with their African sisters in preparing for the future.

Just as help came to Mubende from international sources, an international team dispensed that help in the form of training courses in a variety of fields. On the permanent staff were two Americans and a local Buganda woman. A woman physician from Germany, a British social worker, a Tanganyikan teacher and forty-five Grail members throughout Uganda joined in giving the short courses in health, homecraft, child welfare, agriculture, music and sociology. Fortunately, Mubende is over three thousand miles above sea level, and there is coolness in the heights permitting unremitting work.

"Our Grail Training Center, Mubende," wrote Alice McCarthy, one of the American Grail team, "is a big white house with a red tile roof. It sits in the midst of gardens where we raise most of our food—the bananas and sweet potatoes that are the mainstays of our diet, along with beans, groundnuts and other vegetables."

Besides a year-long course in leadership for a small group of residents, the Center offered eighteen courses of five to ten days to the women of the surrounding countryside.

"Everyone loves the short courses and looks forward to them with enthusiasm. But each one takes careful planning and much hard work. The simple life can be very complicated when you try to house and feed thirty women and seven or eight wailing babies. Our house—at first glance so big—gets smaller and smaller as we fill every square inch with beds and the paraphernalia of living. Many roads are impassable when it rains and so the short courses are held during the dry season. Because we depend entirely on rain water, this can be serious.

"At Christmas last year, when our tanks went dry, we went begging for water. When the tanks around us went dry, we took our 'debbies'—these are the four gallon containers that kerosene comes in and are prized possessions in most East African households—and set off across the road and down the hill to a little stream. This is last-resort water—so dirty and polluted that even after boiling and filtering it stays yellow. It was wet, anyway, so for Christmas everyone had a bonus of a full basin of water."

Women from the villages relish the chance to come to Mubende to discuss their problems, to learn better ways of taking care of their children, of keeping their families well fed and healthy, to learn new skills like cutting out and sewing garments for their families. In discussions they learn about what is going on in the world outside their village, including the activities of the United Nations. So prized are these short courses that one woman hiked over two hundred miles with her baby and her bundles to get to the Grail Training Center.

When the day's studying is done, there are the joys of picnics and dancing, of sharing news of life in the villages of Uganda. Each woman, no matter how poor, pays something for the course—perhaps only a chicken or a few eggs.

Team members at the Center often go out by bicycles and motorcycles to every part of the country—to give lightning courses over a weekend or to remain for a month-long course. During 1960 sixteen courses were held in various parts of the country with eight hundred and thirteen women students. The local planning was done by the Catholic Women's Clubs of Uganda which comprise more than seven thousand women in over three hundred and forty local groups.

The courses are given for women but there are many times

when men are interested spectators. Often village chiefs are invited to the different sessions of the homecraft courses. A recent visitor to Uganda told us of her experience. She was present when the village women practiced bathing a baby under the direction of a nurse. There were women from Buganda and Luo tribal groups. A large negro baby doll sent from the United States was used in the demonstration. Standing in the back of the hall were a group of men, including a local chief.

The women were enthralled. They handled the doll with all seriousness and repeated all the counsels they had received about baby care.

The men looked on with interest and just before the end of the demonstration they were asked for their comments. There was some whispered conversation among them. The chief finally stepped forward to make his considered comment.

"This baby," he stated, "is not a Buganda because his color is wrong. It is too dark."

"It cannot be a Luo. The shape of the head is too round."

"And," he added, "it is neither a boy nor a girl. We do not have that problem in Uganda."

What the leader of the course replied at this point is fortunately, or unfortunately, not known. Such interesting exchanges are never recorded in written reports. However, across the barriers of race and culture, communication of ideas, ideals and hopes is achieved at Mubende.

Tanganyika

Mrs. Robert Hugh Mahoney, as president of the National Council of Catholic Women, was responsible for making the Madonna Plan known throughout the nation. In the pleas which were sent to all NCCW affiliates, she reminded the Catholic women of the United States of the aims of the Madonna Plan:

"Women of the whole world, impelled by our very nature to give life, to protect life, to foster life, can no longer tolerate seeing the frontiers of starvation stamped across our globe in the features of death. . . . Poverty-stricken mothers in many areas of the world need sympathy, understanding and aid. The Madonna Plan of the National Council of Catholic Women aims to mobilize the generosity of American Catholic women to help vitalize the concept of the sacredness of the function of motherhood in areas where it is most threatened . . . It is designed to provide education for young mothers or mothers-to-be in clinics in underdeveloped areas. It is designed to teach these mothers modern hygiene, new and better ways of preparing food so that their children will be healthy and better nourished."

She asked every woman to give a dollar to the cause. "Your dollar will lift a little of the burden that lies on the bodies of so many mothers and their children. Send it at once, won't you, and make a similar contribution next year to continue and expand this work in Mary's name."

During her term of office, Mary Hannan Mahoney became afflicted with a malignant disease that was to take her life. She was a young vigorous woman, full of vitality, and she worked every moment until the illness forced her to a stop. Mary Hannan Mahoney was one of the most complete persons I have ever met. Though she had earned a doctorate in Classical Studies she was interested in all womanly arts—and skilled in them. She would spend her evenings at home sewing garments for the Children in Need drive or for the Papal Storerooms of Charity. On occasions when I dined with Robert and Mary Mahoney at their home in Hartford, Connecticut, she had not only cooked the dinner herself but had baked the bread and rolls that were served with it. Her concern for the welfare of the world community was expressed through all her adult life. As International Relations Chairman for the NCCW she worked closely with its consultant, Miss Catherine Schaeffer, Director of the N.C.W.C. Office for United Nations Affairs. Miss Schaeffer said of her: "Almost inevitably she became chairman of the International Relations Committee and worked tirelessly in it to interest American Catholic women in the Papal Peace Program and in works of charity for the victims of war and oppression."

After she became president in 1956, she carried the message of international charity into every part of the United States. From St. John Chrysostom she culled a quotation which she used in her address to the 1957 World Congress of the Lay Apostolate in Rome. "The most perfect rule of Christianity, its exact definition, its peak, is this: 'seek that which is for the benefit of the community—nothing else can make one more Christ-like than to look after the welfare of others.' Nothing is more useless than a Christian who does not try to save others." This concern for the universal common good was the theme of Mary Mahoney's life and work.

When she could no longer travel physically, she sent her prayers instead. From May to November of 1958, the last few months of her presidency, when the illness was already sapping her strength, she continued to fulfill the tremendous duties involved in that office. The only tasks which she did not perform were long trips—which were forbidden by her doctors. As mentioned in the third chapter, it was because of Mary Mahoney's illness and at her suggestion that I spoke at the convention of Catholic women in Peoria, with the result that Madonna Plan aid went to Indian families through Mother Teresa. Mary Mahoney attended the National Council Convention in St. Louis in November 1958 to finish out her term. Her husband Dr. Robert Hugh Mahoney and her mother Mrs. Jeremiah Hannan were at her side to help keep up her flagging strength.

When she finally had to take to her bed in Georgetown Hospital, she received visitors with the same joy and wit as ever, and asked constantly about the progress of the various activities of the NCCW, particularly the achievements of the Madonna Plan.

On my last visit with Mary Mahoney, on March 17th, 1959, she asked me to tell her where Madonna Plan help had gone. She was delighted to learn that over a score of welfare centers and clinics had received grants and that the five thousand dollars which had been collected by the Scranton Diocesan Council of Catholic Women had gone to aid projects in Africa.

Within a few months, Mary Mahoney was dead. At her funeral Mass in St. Patrick's Church, Washington, D.C., Archbishop Patrick A. O'Boyle in his sermon of eulogy told how her love for the poor and needy was being translated into aid for the most anguished mothers around the world. It was at the time of her death that we learned that Mary Hannan Mahoney had offered up her sufferings for the welfare—spiritual and material—of the people of Tanganyika, especially those in the Diocese of Shinyanga. She knew of the needs of this mission through the Maryknoll bishop, the Most Reverend Edward McGurkin, who came from Hartford and was a close friend of the Mahoneys. To the many people who wanted to send flowers or other memorials at her death, a notice was sent out on behalf of her husband, expressing his wish that in place of flowers, they send an offering for the Madonna Plan. Thousands of dollars came in at once.

Coincidentally, or providentially, it happened that Bishop McGurkin of Shinyanga came to the United States at that time. Part of his mission was to raise funds for a maternity hospital for his area of Tanganyika. Mary Hannan Mahoney's sufferings and death resulted in a first gift of five thousand dollars to help with new life in Africa. The pain of those last months was transmuted into a combined gift of love. Truly no suffering is lost, and truly no Christian is ever powerless, even when helpless and ailing, since prayers can be raised which can be the most powerful means of all.

Bishop McGurkin's plan to build a maternity hospital was changed in favor of several mother and child clinics. In September 1960, His Excellency informed us:

"We already have the Madonna Plan working daily here at the Shinyanga Mission. Mary Mahoney would be very happy (more correctly, *is* very happy) to see this gathering of African mothers and babies getting the expert attention of an American Catholic Sister who is busy at work for them under a Della Robbia 'Madonna' plaque. . . ."

In April of the following year, another progress report came from the bishop, who in the meantime had received more gifts of funds in memory of Mary Mahoney.

"The first *two* maternity clinics in memory of Mary H. Mahoney are nearing completion and we are getting ready to start a third. We have plans for a fourth to get under way before long. Our temporary clinic here in Shinyanga is thronged every morning with mothers and their infants. I am sure that Mary is delighted to see her Madonna Plan bringing relief, hope and joy to these fine people of Tanganyika."

In October, a Quaker leader went to Shinyanga as a "pilgrim in Mary Hannan Mahoney's memory" to see the clinics in operation. He was Thomas R. Bodine, who as a Commissioner of the Housing Authority of Hartford, had been a colleague of Mrs. Mahoney. After attending the triennial meeting of the Friends World Committee in Kenya, Mr. Bodine made his way to Shinyanga. "As the crow flies," or as an airplane would if there had been any airports or planes, the distance was about forty miles. But traveling by jeep over the rough and circuitous road it was more than five hundred. Mr. Bodine carried to Bishop McGurkin the greetings of Dr. Mahoney, Hartford's Superintendent of Schools, who hoped to visit Shinyanga as soon as time permitted.

Mr. Bodine reported on his visit to the clinics and sent us some of the photographs he had taken there. In one picture with Mr. Bodine is a handsome young African mother, with a serene, confident expression, holding in her arms a plump healthy baby. Above her head is a Della Robbia plaque, a symbol of all motherhood and of its infinite sacredness. Under the plaque were the words: "The Mary Hannan Mahoney Memorial Maternity Clinic."

In successive years, Dr. Robert H. Mahoney devoted his summers to pilgrimages of charity in memory of his wife. Reporting back to women's groups on the progress of the Mary Hannan Mahoney Memorial Clinics, soon numbering seven, he raised funds for their operation and expansion.

I thought of Mary dying, and in her pain praying that others might live more fully, and I remembered those words of St. Paul, ". . . as dying, and behold we live."

San Salvador—Inn of the Madonna

"It is heart-stopping. Not only do the mothers have to beg, but the children hold out their hands for food from the time they can walk. At night, many of these mothers and children don't even have a hut to creep into. They lie down in the open streets, in the gutters, anywhere that they find themselves at the end of the day. It is the one thing that bothers me most about San Salvador.

"I hope I can get Madonna Plan help for our city. Isn't the Madonna Plan set up to emphasize the dignity of all motherhood? I am banking on the National Council of Catholic Women."

Joseph Battaglia had come to New York from San Salvador. He was Program Director for the Catholic Relief Services Mission to El Salvador, the smallest and most densely populated republic of Central America. After nearly a decade of civilian and refugee relief work with the agency in Germany, he had volunteered to serve in Latin America when his office in Munich was closed.

After his years of personal contact with some of the bleakest refugee camps in Western Europe, Mr. Battaglia found himself in an entirely different situation. Here there were no refugees and no camps, but need spilled out into the open streets. There was little or no public assistance or any kind of welfare system to dole out a subsistence in money, clothing or food. Only the loveliness of the city of San Salvador softened the impact of the extreme misery. Fanciful local architecture in brilliant colors of blue, pink and beige glowed under the bright sunlight. Great palm and banana trees offered little oases of dark shade.

In this new environment, Joseph Battaglia pitched in to meet new challenges. Concentrating on the strengthening of the local Caritas, or Catholic Charities organization, he had in less than two years helped to establish a crucially important supplementary feeding program which reached a quarter of a million people in El Salvador. The program also included three hundred and fifty thousand needy school children in a massive school lunch network. From American abundance, tortillas, cheese and milk were channeled to El Salvador's needy in an operation that utilized the skill and good will of thousands of Salvadorans.

In a country like El Salvador, where fifty cents is the daily wage on the coffee plantations, there is no social security, no pension plan. It is not surprising therefore that thousands trek to the capital where, on the busy streets, their begging hands can at least receive a few coins from the passers-by.

"The local people have done wonders in the past couple of years," Mr. Battaglia told us. "Caritas is ready to undertake a census of the poor so that we will know just what the total problem is. We have a fine Women's Economic Committee working with Caritas, and just recently, a Junior Economic Committee has been formed. The Salvadoran teenagers are getting deeply involved in the program.

"We are almost ready to set up a new service for the homeless mothers and children. The government has given a good-sized mansion just for this purpose. A team of Religious Sisters is ready to live at the center to give all sorts of aid.

"And that's not all," Mr. Battaglia continued. "The Mayor of San Salvador has contributed the kitchen equipment. Voluntary kitchen help will come from the *Club Familiar,* a self-help project of the needy themselves. Sewing machines already sent by Madonna Plan will be the basis for a sewing school—and we can work on clothing donated in the Thanksgiving Clothing Campaign. The women will be free to follow the course because two *Guardarias,* day nurseries, will take the little children while their mothers are being trained.

"But running expenses we don't have and can't find. Before we can open, we need the assurance of running expenses for a year. I had pinned my hopes on the Madonna Plan. We already have a small income from the sale of flour bags, so two hundred dollars a month from the Madonna Plan would do it. If we had three hundred dollars a month, we could also open up a clinic. These mothers need a lot of health care before they can be rehabilitated."

I took down all that Joseph Battaglia had said, but I knew that Madonna Plan funds were too low at the moment to include this project.

Soon after this conversation, a long-distance call from Toledo and a letter from Mrs. Margaret Zemo, Foreign Relief Secretary of the NCCW in Washington, came on the same day. The women of the Toledo Diocesan Council of Catholic Women wanted to sponsor a specific Madonna Plan project to honor Mrs. Arthur L. Zepf on her retirement as President of the NCCW. Elizabeth Zepf's devotion to the Foreign Relief program had inspired the women of her diocese to honor her by supporting an overseas charity. The Toledo women wanted this support to start immediately.

I hurriedly described the San Salvador center. The money was pledged at once, and word was sent to Mr. Battaglia.

Within a few weeks the shelter was opened. The name given to it was the Elizabeth Ann Zepf Posada de la Madonna. *Posada* has the meaning of shelter or inn.

We received pictures of the Salvadorans who were being fed daily through this program. Three hundred women and their children were served in three daily sittings. In the photographs we saw two young Georgetown University student nurses at work among the women. They were spending their summer vacation volunteering at the shelter—bathing babies encrusted with dirt, caring for minor ailments, helping the mothers choose clean garments. The two young women, Maureen Barrett of Buffalo, New York, and Joana Vinti of New Jersey, had much to tell their classmates during the winter term in Washington, D.C.

Joana Vinti came to Catholic Relief Services to tell me some of her impressions of that summer. She was one of twenty-four girls who had volunteered to spend their holidays doing social welfare work in El Salvador. The talks given by Joseph Battaglia had moved members of the Young Christian Workers to make a joint assault on the misery of one Central American country. Father Edward Cooke of Ramsey, New Jersey, had helped galvanize the whole summer effort. All of the girls had paid their own fares to perform the works of charity of teaching, administering the feeding program, and nursing.

"It was hard work," Joana said. "Bathing those little babies was fun, though. They are lovely children when you get the grime off and get them into some fresh clothing. The food is helping them a lot. You should see their poor mothers. Their sufferings show up in their faces."

She took out a snapshot. "How old do you think this woman is?" she asked, pointing to a woman standing outside the *posada*.

"She certainly looks middle-aged," I answered. "Her face is so drawn and lined. But you know, I worked in Calcutta, and there a poor widow looks like a crone at forty."

Joana nodded reflectively. "This may be worse than Calcutta. This woman is an old crone at twenty-eight. I made a habit of asking them their ages, and I was shocked every time. Women in their thirties have the faces of sixty-year-olds."

"But do you have hope that things are going to be better now?" I asked.

"Definitely," Joana replied. "Young girls from the local schools are taking up where we left off. That was the best part of our summer's experience. As we were leaving, the clinic was ready to start, with a doctor and a nurse on regular service."

Once more, NCCW-Madonna Plan had forged a bond of unity based on personal contact. To San Salvador flew Elizabeth Zepf in the spring of 1965. Of the days she spent at the Inn of the Madonna, she wrote: "As the women gathered round me, and I learned of their heartbreaking problems, I kept saying prayers of thanks that my name had been attached to this work of rescue. I felt so humble, because any one of them might have been me. The tears that filled my eyes were not only tears of sadness. They were tears of gratitude, too, for the fact that Madonna Plan could be a channel of hope to women who had been deprived even of their personal dignity."

Colombia

In Colombia, the Madonna Plan gave aid to two projects that showed the way to the solution of one of Latin America's deepest problems—the class structure. This cuts through the bonds of Christian charity by tending to stratify people on separate levels and tends to becloud the traditional Christian teaching on the use of property, which binds a Christian to share his goods with his brother.

The effect of the complete separation of classes is that the upper class tends to assume that its own needs are almost infinite, and all extras and luxuries should be utilized for its comfort. The rationalization is that the lower classes, lacking culture and the refinements of life, would not know what to do with such items as plumbing, higher education, privacy, and all the other qualities of the good life.

Where the classes of a society are kept apart, the poor get poorer, while the rich and propertied get richer—this has happened in Latin America. In this atmosphere even Christian benevolence can serve to emphasize the gap between the classes—only one class giving, the other able only to receive. There is no real meeting on the level of human equality set down by Christ.

The two projects in Colombia to which NCCW funds were now channeled were examples of a more Christian concept of sharing. In the first, a widow who had space in her house to share and talents to extend used them on behalf of children and families in a society torn apart by years of violence. In the other, a country priest in a village on a steep hillside outside of Bogota, starting with no funds and an old radio transmitter, shared the fruits of the spirit with millions locked in the prison of ignorance and isolation in the remotest villages of his country.

They also call me mama

Mrs. Edward Shea, the Catholic Relief Services Project Supervisor for Latin America, told me about this remarkable woman called Mama Fanny. Besides creating homes for more than two hundred and fifty children, she was engaged in building training schools for these boys and girls, and in promoting a housing development for homeless families. A whole quarter, called the *Barrio de Jesus de la Buena Esperanza,* was growing in Pereira—twenty-eight houses were the work of a housing committee on which Senora Fanny served as President.

Her full name was Doña Fanny Aristizabal de Arenas.

We learned that she was coming to visit her married daughter who lived in New York City. In our office, we asked her to tell us how she came to be so involved in the conditions of her country.

She asked us: "Can you picture a city—not a big city—that needs a dormitory to shelter homeless children picked up on the streets at night? One of these is essential in Pereira. I worked to start this dormitory because the children were curling up in corners of the streets like abandoned little animals.

"Have you ever met a four-year old boy who saw his mother and father beheaded by bandits—who was found with his smaller brothers in a pool of their blood? Thank God you have never seen, as I have, ten-year old homeless girls placed in hotels for prostitution. Have you seen whole families, innocent and confused, arrive from the countryside with no money and no hope of work or shelter? These are things I have seen—and much more—on the streets of my city and on the roads of our poor countryside. This is what drives me to carry on this work. This is why my own home was the first shelter for wandering children."

"When did you start taking children into your own household?" we asked her, knowing that she lived in a section of Colombia particularly affected by violence occasioned by a political split in the government. Once this had broken out in the towns, it quickly spread to the countryside. A chain of violence began in which every murder was answered with reprisal, and bandits prolonged the chaos and kept the blood flowing.

"Families from the country came fleeing into Pereira," she told us. "Then we saw children wandering about. But we thought that they had their mother or father with them. One night on my way home from a movie I saw several children sleeping on a doorstep in a heavy rain. After I went home I started to think about all of them sleeping out there—almost under my own doorstep. It hurt my heart so that I could not go to bed. I got up and went out again and gathered all the children that I found. I came back with five of them, and this was the beginning. . . .

"After I had talked with my sons, we began to look for a piece of land to start a home not only for the five who lived with us permanently, but for the others that I gathered every night.

"Providence answered our prayers. A generous man donated a piece of land, a farm property near Pereira. We put some money in, and the money grew. On the land we built the first of the *granje infantil*—children's shelter. We called it the *Granje Infantil de Jesus de la Buena Esperanza*—the Children's Shelter of Jesus of Good Hope. In the boys' shelter are nearly a hundred boys. They are from five to fifteen years old. My ideal is to have a place for every child in need of a home, to make good men out of these little ones—they are wild like animals not by their own fault. We want to help make them persons that society will be proud of, to educate not only their minds, but to teach them to be useful and to earn a living. We will have training in carpentry and shoe-making.

"The teaching Sisters, Las Madres de la Enseñanza, have now taken over the girls' shelter. It is not finished completely, but it has a dormitory and classrooms. There is a residence for the Sisters and a chapel.

"We are grateful to Catholic Relief Services and to CARE for food from North America. What would we do for our family of children if we did not have rice, and flour, and corn and powdered milk? But the family is growing. We received enough for a hundred, and now we have to feed two hundred and fifty children.

"You know that I work with the poor families of Pereira, especially the mothers. We have even been able to start a little housing project for homeless families. For them it is almost impossible to get medical help even in an emergency. Some sort of medical help would be important for all our poor—the families and the homeless children."

Doña Fanny said that she could locate a room that could be used as a consulting room. It might be a long time before a real clinic with a full-time doctor could be established, so in the meantime it was decided that from Madonna Plan funds a full-time nurse would be supplied. An extra grant would pay for the regular visit of a doctor. The nurse would give first-aid treatment and keep records for the doctor. This could be done for twelve hundred dollars a year and medicines could be channeled through our regular program. Doña Fanny returned to Pereira to engage a nurse with Madonna Plan aid.

A few months later pictures arrived of the people served by the medical team. One snapshot showed a mother and her newborn baby with the smiling father and a nurse. On the back was written:

Matrimonia Campesino—La mama y el nino se salvaran gracias al medico y enfermera que Uds tan generosoa mente nos estan agando.

Que Dios les pague. Fanny Aristizabal.

Rural couple—the mother and child were saved thanks to the doctor and nurse for whom you are so generously paying.

May God repay you. Fanny Aristizabal.

Light breaks into the "anti-hygienic fortresses"

In an adobe hut in a village high up in the Andes mountains of Colombia, a small group of women are sitting around
a table waiting for a signal. Conversation has stopped, and
there is an air of expectation. They are peasant women, gathered in the house of one of their members. A blackboard has
been set up against the wall next to the vivid posters showing
Colombian mothers and their babies.

On the crude table are two objects, an alarm clock and a
radio receiving set. It is six o'clock in the evening. Suddenly
the shrill sound of the alarm breaks the stillness. This is the
signal the women have been awaiting. The alarm tells them
it's time to turn on a special battery-operated transmitter
radio.

The voice of Dr. Alejandro Salas, chief of the Health Sec-
tion of *Radio Sutatenza,* begins a discussion of *La Madre y El
Nino*—The Mother and Child. It is the opening talk of the
Cursillo de la Madre y El Nino. There will be thirty lectures
in the simplest, most direct language, one every Saturday,
Sunday and Monday for ten weekends.

The subjects are to include: "From Healthy Parents are
Born Healthy Children"; "Take Care of Your Health for the
Welfare of Your Child"; "Prepare for the Baby." The last
lecture is to be "Children are the Images of God."

During his first talk, Dr. Salas makes a special announce-
ment: "For the first time, the Madonna Plan of the National
Council of Catholic Women of North America is cooperating
with the *Radio Sutatenza* program for the mother and child."

Each week the mothers who listen to the talks will fill out a
questionnaire appearing in the weekly paper, *El Campesino.*
On the last questionnaire she will fill in the ages of her chil-

dren as well as her name and address. All of the forms will be mailed by the monitor to *Radio Sutatenza* headquarters near Bogota. Those whose answers show the best understanding of the course will receive gifts of new clothing: if the mother has a newborn baby, she will receive a layette; if her children are older she will receive other types of garments. They are among those donated to the Holy Father for his Storerooms of Charity in Vatican City. The Holy Father in turn made his gifts available to needy mothers and children around the world and Colombia is one of the countries benefited.

The women sitting around the table were some of the thousands who tuned in to *Radio Sutatenza* for the first lecture of *El Cursillo de la Madre y El Nino.*

In every course the setup was the same—a battery-operated radio receiving set, a blackboard, graphic posters and most probably an alarm clock. The radio set could tune in only one station—*Radio Sutatenza,* the school system pioneered by Monsignor José Joaquin Salcedo of the village of Sutatenza, Colombia.

When Monsignor Salcedo, whose primary concern was instructing the ignorant of Colombia, heard of the Madonna Plan of the National Council of Catholic Women, he said it would fit in with "our radiofonic health campaign." Miss Teresa Parada, a young Colombian woman on the staff of his New York office, accordingly forwarded Dr. Salas' report to NCCW headquarters.

Before long we were in touch with Dr. Salas and had learned about his courses on hygiene and health for the mother and child. These were couched in the most basic terms so that mothers who had little or no education could profit by them.

Radio Sutatenza and its founder, Monsignor Salcedo, have

become known through various articles and studies. UNESCO, for example, pointed to *Radio Sutatenza* as an outstanding effort in the field of fundamental education. In an on-the-spot survey made by UNESCO in 1960, it was estimated that seven hundred and forty-nine thousand people took part in some course given in the *Radio Sutatenza* educational program. At that time there were in operation some forty-six thousand four hundred radio sets capable of receiving the Sutatenza broadcast.

The man who put this enormous radio school system in motion, was a thin dynamic priest who in his early teens had been a radio "ham." Even when he went on to the seminary, he continued tinkering with radios in his spare time and was called by his fellow students the "Don Quixote of the Radio."

Upon his ordination he was assigned to the tiny village of Sutatenza in the high Colombian Andes. The people of Sutatenza, less than one hundred in number, and those of the surrounding villages, all served by the same pastor, had to make their living by crops grown on the steep, eroded slopes. Some raised a few athletic sheep. Some were able to cultivate coffee. In the unremitting struggle for bare survival, the *campesinos* of the Andes had little outlet except in alcohol.

Young Father Salcedo decided to give the village *taberna* some competition. He built a primitive radio transmitter and with vacationing seminarians began tests to see how far his radio announcements would reach into the mountains. He then began to record the voices of laborers who were working far from their home villages. After he had placed a few receiving sets in these villages he broadcasted the messages of the men to their families. The marvel set tongues buzzing; the countryside was excited at this "new" type of communication.

Now Father Salcedo was ready to start his campaign—a campaign to force entry into the dark, windowless adobe huts of the *campesinos*. He appealed to his people for gifts of a single chicken toward a new transmitter and some receiving sets. Hundreds of chickens were brought to Sunday Mass, and these were trucked to Bogota and sold. With the money from these sales, the "Don Quixote of the Radio" purchased from American Army surplus a used two hundred and fifty watt transmitter and radio receivers for fifteen villages.

Father Salcedo immediately put this system to use by beginning a course in reading and writing for the illiterate villagers. It was necessary to have a person who was literate to serve as monitor for the class. Thus was born a system of choosing an *auxiliar*, or monitor, from the village itself. It was the task of the local pastor to locate a suitable *auxiliar* who would repeat the letters that came over the radio and lead the group in writing them down. It worked out that a person of normal intelligence could learn basic literacy in six months through *Radio Sutatenza*.

From the initial transmitter, Father Salcedo built up a broadcasting system which utilized a dozen powerful transmitters. As the number of persons taking his courses grew, he needed a corps of trained *Auxiliares*. He began to arrange courses for monitors at Sutatenza, bringing in groups of eager learners and sending them back to their villages trained in the fundamentals of teaching and community development. He called the whole movement, *Accion Cultural Popular*, Popular Cultural Action. The "Don Quixote of the Radio" had tilted his beam at the seemingly impregnable "adobe fortresses" and had breached them by the thousands and then by the tens of thousands.

In the wake of the courses, and of a drop in illiteracy from seventy-four to forty percent in some areas of Colombia, a new need developed for simple practical literature on basic subjects. As such literature did not exist, *Radio Sutatenza* set up an efficient printing press in Bogota. Manuals of agriculture, health and the fundamentals of Christian life and belief appeared. A catechism, *Creo en Dios,* geared to the needs of *Radio Sutatenza's* listeners, was produced and distributed widely. These manuals formed the *Biblioteca Campesina* placed in villages all over Colombia.

A second cooperative effort of the Madonna Plan-NCCW and Popular Cultural Action grew out of the printing establishment. The lectures of Dr. Alejandro Salas had such a wide and interested audience that it was decided to print them in an illustrated manual. A Madonna Plan grant was offered for the publication of the *Cursillo de la Madre y El Nino.*

Dr. Salas decided that as the manual should be sold or bartered, the Madonna Plan grant should be used to cover only about two-thirds of the cost of the publication of a booklet in two colors. The first printing numbered sixty thousand copies. The booklet carried a colorful Andean family on its cover and a tribute to "Madonna Plan del Consejo Nacional de las Mujeres Catolicas des los Estados Unidos" on the back cover. Through Catholic Relief Services the booklet was sent to every country in Latin America, to be shared with clinics and training centers for the mother and child.

The first copies went to the *Bibliotecas Campesinas* and parish houses throughout rural Colombia. A second means of distribution were the rural markets and stores. As chickens played a key role in starting *Radio Sutatenza,* so they continued to play a role in the promotion of its educational efforts. The *campesina,* who rarely had money to spare, could obtain a copy of the manual by bringing one fresh egg to the store. The storekeeper would sell the egg, take a ten-percent commission on the sale, and return the rest of the proceeds to *Radio Sutatenza.*

Radio Sutatenza continued to find ways to adapt technology and promotional methods to meet human needs; it tried to confront the deepest and most pressing problems of Latin American life. One of its aims was to stem the uncontrolled exodus of rural people to the cities by fostering respect for the vocation of farming and by making rural life more meaningful. Very soon its example was followed in other Latin American countries facing the same problem. Radio St. Gabriel in Bolivia, the "Voice of the Andes" in Ecuador, Radio Schools for Literacy in Peru, the Radio Schools in Brazil and the Faith and Joy Schools in Venezuela, all learned from the Sutatenza experiment. This was the beginning of the attack on the illiteracy which plagues at least eighty million of Latin America's poorest.

As with *Radio Sutatenza,* so with other continuing projects throughout the world, the Madonna Plan was able to help large and important projects in little ways—in ways that had meaning not only for those who were served but for those in the United States who were serving.

Aid reached the mothers of Quemoy Island, helping to maintain a kindergarten for their children. Father Druetto, the representative of Catholic Relief Services on Quemoy, had begun the kindergarten in order to give the mothers some extra time to rebuild the homes shattered in shellfire from China's mainland. Refugee mothers from China who reached Macao were given medical care by the Franciscan Missionaries of Mary at the Pius XII Social Center built with the aid of Catholic Relief Services. A Madonna Plan grant went to the Sisters at this strategic spot on the Bamboo Curtain. In Penampang, North Borneo, the Sisters of St. Joseph received a small grant to help them with their maternity home and clinic.

To Asia, Africa, Latin America, went the love and concern of Catholic women—even to such holy places as Jerusalem and Bethlehem. By the time Madonna Plan reached its fifth year of operation, close to a hundred centers around the world had benefited from Madonna Plan aid. Grants of help reached the White Sisters while they were operating inside the Casbah of Algiers. Though ordered to quit the Casbah the Sisters continued to serve the Kabyle mothers in Algerian villages. One of the Sisters put into words what seemed to be the real significance of the Madonna Plan help, limited as it might be:

"This Madonna Plan aid in Algeria has been extremely important, not merely for the assistance—material and moral—given to the mother and child clinics, but even more important in being a concrete testimonial of the interest Catholic women of the United States have in the role of the mother in the proper development of society and in the sacredness of human life."

Madonna Plan as trailblazer

Often, small Madonna Plan gifts served as "seed money" for much larger grants from other sources. A case in point was the grant made available to the Catholic Social Center on the island of Dominica in the British West Indies. Part of the grant went to pay for a social worker at the center, from which services and community activities were developed not only for Dominica, but for adjoining islands as well. The moving spirit behind the whole project was Sister Mary Alicia of the Missionaries of St. Augustine whose little known work gradually became better known. The Catholic women of England learned of the achievements in the community development promoted by the Social League of Catholic Women in Dominica. They sponsored a collection for this work, during which more than forty-seven thousand English pounds poured in for these programs. A letter from the Catholic Social Center in Dominica told us: "In view of this gift from Britain, we find it only right to cancel our request to you for help from the Madonna Plan . . . We are extremely grateful to the Madonna Plan. Your help has certainly brought us through a crisis."

A grant to a Mexican Catholic agency serving the native Indian villages had the effect of pointing a finger at good work performed in a remote area. The aid went to supplement the nutrition of Otomi Indians living on some of the most arid and poorest land in all Mexico. During the course of the first year's grant it was possible to raise the nutritional level of hundreds of Otomi families through the addition of protein foods to their diets. Health, energy and working power showed improvement. A social worker supplied quarterly reports that were sent to Catholic Relief Headquarters along with the regular reports of the Mexico Mission of the agency. These reports were shared not only with the Washington headquarters of the NCCW, but also with the Geneva office, from which information was disseminated to various European voluntary agencies. In many cases these agencies were anxious to bring some aid to other continents. The British agency, Oxford Famine Relief Committee, became interested in the work being done with the Indians and gave a significant grant to the Mexican agency to allow it to enlarge its nutritional services to the Otomi and other inhabitants of Mexico.

Perhaps the most dramatic example of "trailblazing" by

the Madonna Plan was the help that went to Mother Teresa and the Missionaries of Charity, as related in the third chapter of this book. Mother Teresa had been helped in various ways by Catholic Relief Services, especially with bulk foods that were channeled to Calcutta's most famished citizens. Among the first, if not the first, aid in funds that reached her from overseas was the Madonna Plan grant from the Peoria Diocese. Once some interest was aroused, notice in the American press followed. At our suggestion, *Jubilee* Magazine arranged for Mother Teresa's activities to be photographed. Several picture stories had the effect of eliciting widespread giving to strengthen the works of the Missionaries of Charity.

Other diocesan councils followed in the trail of Peoria in adopting specific programs of the Missionaries of Charity. When a team of Indian Missionaries of Charity journeyed to Venezuela to take up work in the State of Yaracuy, the Brooklyn Diocesan Council of Catholic Women sponsored the whole program. Mrs. Leo Sartan, Foreign Relief Chairman for the Brooklyn Archdiocese, asked me to give her all the data possible on the needs in Venezuela. On a week's inspection trip into the interior with Mother Teresa, I took films of life in small villages in the rich forest land around the towns of San Felipe and Cocorote. These Venezuelans, descendants of African slaves, were not sharing in the good things that were becoming a part of life around them. Their bishop heard of the work of Mother Teresa at the Vatican Council, and invited her to bring a team of Indian Sisters to his diocese of Barquisimeto. The intermediary was the Internuncio to India, the Most Reverend R. J. Knox.

Warmhearted people, dark-skinned and strong, welcomed Mother Teresa as she made quick stops in village after village. When the team of Sisters arrived some months later, the townspeople put their arms out to the darkest of the group, saying, "These are our very own Sisters. We have been waiting for them."

As rupees could not be brought out of India, Mother Teresa had to locate sponsors for this dramatic work, in which a mission country was bearing fruit and sending Indian Sisters for the first time to the New World. Helen Sartan told the story to the women of Brooklyn and put Madonna Boxes as reminders at every meeting. Thousands of dollars mounted up as the boxes were emptied and their contents sent to NCCW headquarters. These donations were translated into medicines, sewing machines and other needs as specified by the Missionaries of Charity in Venezuela.

As a memorial of Mother Teresa's visit to Nevada, the women of the Diocese of Reno gathered a donation of one thousand dollars for the Venezuelan mission.

Following the NCCW meeting in Las Vegas, it was my privilege to accompany Mother Teresa to Europe. It was a happy development that her appearance at the national convention of American Catholic women provided the opportunity for her to explain her work to a half dozen European voluntary societies concerned with overseas aid.

Our first stop in Europe was London, and our first call was made on the Oxford Famine Relief Committee. Canon T. R. Milford, for the Committee, questioned Mother Teresa regarding her most urgent needs. She explained that her great desire, while in England, was to obtain a supply of an anti-leprosy medicine produced by the ICI, Imperial Chemical Industries. She told of the beneficial results she and others had had in using this medicament on lepers in the *bustees*, or slum settlements, that ringed Calcutta. Doctors trained in the treatment of Hansen's disease worked with the Missionaries of Charity in a program that carried help and relief to the destitute lepers of the refugee-packed metropolis.

After a few more questions Canon Milford told Mother Teresa: "The order will be placed in London, and the supplies for your lepers will be released to you through the Calcutta office of the chemical company. When you have used a given amount, you can renew the order and we will arrange the payment from here."

The efficacy of the Geneva office of Catholic Relief Services was never better demonstrated than during Mother Teresa's two-week stay on the continent. We kept appointments with Misereor, the German Bishops Overseas Aid Committee in Aachen, with the leaders of the Rice for Calcutta Collection in Cologne, with Swiss Caritas in Lucerne, with Swiss Overseas Aid in Berne.

Mother Teresa did not plead in human terms for the lepers, the homeless, the destitute dying. She told her listeners of the plight her people found themselves in, and then repeated her simple invitation, "Here is a chance for you to do something beautiful for God." She referred, as always, to the poor and afflicted as "Christ in the distressing disguise of need." Her very presence was a call to conscience. As a result of that presence, more than half a million dollars in help was immediately pledged to her for continued help to the afflicted of India.

5

Feed-A-Family help for the most threatened families

In the twentieth century, the family has been threatened as never before—by persecution, wars, mass expulsions, long exile, upheaval, unremitting hunger and revolution. Families have been fragmented; the ties with the past have been severed.

Revolutionaries have always realized that to inculcate a new set of political values, the family, as conserver of the old values, must be weakened and broken up. Thus, newly-imposed Marxist regimes pit children against their parents as spies and critics. In the new China, the family system, one of the strongest in the world, was weakened by the substitution of a system of communal living. In a tribute to the basic and irreplaceable necessity of the family, the more established Marxist regimes have restored the family to a stronger place in their way of life.

As the family is the basis on which the individual perceives an image of himself and of the ideal person he might be, this image is threatened when the family disintegrates. The up-rooted, weakened family can leave children with no effective image of themselves, no clear-cut goals or ideals. When we see that throughout the world millions of families have been shattered, we can realize how many of the children become the rootless, humiliated, resentful people who form a sort of sub-proletariat to the productive economy of the world.

History teaches us that those who feel themselves outside society, who do not share in the goods or goals of their time or place, are the ones who can be drawn into movements to subvert its accepted order. They become revolutionaries not only to establish a better social order, but also to work out their deep resentments. They have nothing to lose, since they are convinced that nothing could be worse than their own situation. If there is a new order, they at least will enjoy the use of some directive power. They will no longer be passive victims.

All over the world, the programs of Catholic Relief Services-N.C.W.C. were directed to rebuilding the ruins of the most threatened families. This was so in Western Europe, in enclaves of refugees in the Middle East, India and Paki-stan, Vietnam, Hong Kong and Korea. Working with local agencies and hundreds of thousands of local volunteers, our agency poured in funds, clothing and foods to bring emer-gency aid to homeless and exiled family groups. After the period of emergency aid was over, every effort was made to promote housing, jobs and training to help restore to the family some of the dignity of which it had been robbed.

Catholic Relief Services-N.C.W.C. was one of the Ameri-can people-to-people agencies which urged the government of the United States to channel its massive food surpluses to the needy overseas. In statement after statement we joined with other such agencies in urging legislators and administrators in Washington to make wheat, corn, powdered milk, dried eggs, beans and oils available not only to the governments of needy countries, but also to voluntary agencies. These could in turn distribute the food among refugees who would not otherwise be reached either by national or international organizations.

Joining with twenty-one other voluntary agencies, including church-related groups such as Church World Service, Lutheran World Relief and the American Jewish Joint Distribution Committee, Catholic Relief Services participated in the distribution of more than nine billion pounds of American grain and dairy products in eighty-two countries and areas of the world, during the 1950's.

But the ration of surplus food given to each family was often not sufficient to keep them alive. Certainly there were needs other than food for refugees in Hong Kong for example, and for the near four million Koreans who fled south of the 38th Parallel into a denuded land. It was for such supplementary needs that the Feed-A-Family program of the NCCW provided.

In 1957 when the World Union of Catholic Women's Organizations had its meeting in Rome, the American affiliate was asked to report on the Feed-A-Family program as one example of an activity which was an effective part of the War Against Hunger. Miss Margaret Mealey, Executive Director of the NCCW, gave the report to the Catholic women leaders of the world.

The item of greatest interest to the women of other countries, who knew more about hunger than Americans, was the manner in which world needs were brought home to the women in the parishes; the methods that could be utilized to acquaint a woman in Albuquerque, New Mexico, with the problems of a needy family in Pusan, Korea.

Miss Mealey stressed the role of the monthly bulletin of the NCCW. This publication carried to nearly twenty thousand women regular articles on the Foreign Relief Committee. The articles, prepared on the basis of material supplied by the consultant to the committee, detailed different aspects of world needs, and showed how women could alleviate these needs through one of the foreign relief programs of NCCW. She mentioned also the other ways in which word reached the individual woman so as to arouse her compassionate help.

One of the functions of the consultant at the headquarters of Catholic Relief Services-N.C.W.C. was the preparation of the series of pamphlets entitled "The Works of Peace." These pamphlets, carrying on the front page the dove of peace, gave the women firsthand reports, either from the consultant's own experience, or from the experiences of the various Catholic Relief Services representatives, of need in anguished areas of the world. Local diocesan and parish groups often reprinted the materials supplied to them, and used them in talks and in local promotion.

Two documentary movies helped to tell the story of human need. Both were prepared by this author in conjunction with a professional film-maker. One was entitled "The Works of Peace," and gave actual scenes of Catholic Relief Services representatives at work around the world with groups of refugees. Through the help of news cameramen in the field for the National Broadcasting Company, film footage was obtained from Europe, the Middle East and Asia. This was combined with scenes from newsreels to round out the graphic picture of events.

A second film, "Pilgrimage of Grace," dealt with the exodus and resettlement of the refugees from North Vietnam. The news footage of the war in Vietnam gave dramatic background to the actual scenes of the arrival of refugees in Hanoi and their transport to Saigon. Then came scenes of emergency help in Saigon, and the unceremonious trucking of the refugees out to the rural areas. Unforgettable scenes, filmed by cameramen of the United States Information Agency, showed the Vietnamese cutting away the underbrush, building their simple homes, planting their first gardens, and working in the cooperatives founded with help from Catholic Relief Services. These films were shown for many years, and one could always see the human need in the faces of those enduring their hour of suffering.

In addition to material prepared by our agency and by the NCCW, other concerned persons championed the cause of foreign relief. Chief among these was Mrs. Katherine Burton, who time and time again gave the brilliance of her pen to stimulating the works of charity among American women. Her columns in *The Sign* magazine, under the title "Woman to Woman," never failed to produce a wave of generosity. No sooner had the monthly issue of *The Sign* reached its readers throughout the country than the shower of checks and money gifts came to the Feed-A-Family program, the Madonna Plan or the Help-A-Child program. All three programs were described in unforgettable terms in Mrs. Burton's column. To her, and to her gift of expression, the National Council of Catholic Women and Catholic Relief Services-N.C.W.C. are in deep debt.

Christmas time was an occasion to remind people of the needs of others and of the obligation of charity. Christmas cards were sold for the benefit of the Feed-A-Family program. These were first designed by Monsignor Lawrence Ernst,

Moderator of the Toledo Diocesan Council of Catholic Women. The Foreign Relief Chairman, Mrs. Arthur Zepf, was from the Toledo Diocese, and was helped in her apostolate of overseas charity by the inventiveness and indefatigable support of Msgr. Ernst. Through him, the women had access to a fine printing press and, after printing special Feed-A-Family donation envelopes (the Toledo Diocese was an outstanding leader in financial support of the program), Msgr. Ernst experimented with a Feed-A-Family Christmas Card. The card was such a success in the diocese that it was accepted as a national program. During World Refugee Year, the card carried, besides the usual Christmas greeting and a representation of the Holy Family, the following message:

"This card represents a donation to the Feed-A-Family program of the National Council of Catholic Women. In cooperation with Catholic Relief Services-N.C.W.C. the program reaches some of the neediest families—especially refugees—in twelve areas around the globe.

"THROUGH THIS GIFT, DURING WORLD REFUGEE YEAR, HELP WILL REACH A NEEDY FAMILY IN THE NAME OF THE HOLY FAMILY WHO ONCE WERE REFUGEES."

The Rome meeting of the World Union of Catholic Women provided a means of dramatizing the needs of the family of man. An historic pageant was presented in the Church of the Gesu entitled "The Hungers of Mankind." Mrs. Mary Mahoney who attended this conference as President of the NCCW, gave us a report on "The Hungers of Mankind" and on the inspiration it gave to continue the Feed-A-Family program. She concluded her report with these words:

"As your delegate . . . I report this prayerful petition for the Hungers of Mankind. What can we do to relieve them? . . .

"To relieve such distress, you and I, through the Catholic Relief Services, can send the NCCW Feed-A-Family parcels which have been gratefully termed bags of gold because of their welcome contents."

Mrs. Mahoney's appeal was distributed throughout the country—and "The Hungers of Mankind" pageant was presented in many cities of the United States.

Korea

Korea is a case in point for the operation of the women's "War Against Hunger" through the Feed-A-Family program. It was one of sixteen countries where dedicated men and women, on the front lines of that massive year-in, year-out war, were given the only weapon that mattered to them, food for the starving.

I visited Korea in 1955 and saw some of the war's effects on family life. Close to half a million bereft, confused women were war widows. The cities were ringed with countless thousands of shacks thrown together from rice bags, cardboard, tin and any piece of salvageable scrap material. The busiest Koreans of those days were the men, women and children who searched endlessly in the mounds of waste material thrown out by the city and by U.S. Army depots. Old packing cases of every size and description were prize finds. They were the basis for a new wall of a shack, or for a few fires to cut the edge of the arctic cold.

In Pusan, the clinic of the Maryknoll Sisters served close to a thousand patients every day. At four A.M. the line began to form outside the clinic, to wait until the Sisters began their long day at 7:30. I saw the suffering Koreans patiently waiting for a little alleviation of their pain. There were old men and women barely able to walk the few steps to the consulting room; children crippled with tuberculosis of the bone; people afflicted with all sorts of skin diseases and some with the signs of leprosy. There were men and women hunched over as if in extreme pain. I noticed one boy who had a scarred, blistered face that was a deep blue color and asked one of the Sisters about him. She explained that the boy had burned his face, and that his family had smeared ink all over the burned areas as first-aid. Koreans believe ordinary ink to be an anti-burn medicine.

As I made my way through the Clinic, I heard the repeated greeting of peace, *"An yan ha simnika?"* "Is there peace with you?" This was the greeting throughout the centuries when Korea as the "Hermit Kingdom" had cut itself off from international contacts. During this time the Koreans called their country "The land of the morning calm," and turned aside from every entanglement with other peoples. After a forty-year occupation by Japan, the peninsular nation was caught up in the violent whirlwind of modern history, and was ultimately left in a shambles. The word *An,* meaning peace, sounded tragic, coming as it did from the mouths of these victims of war.

Before leaving the clinic, I went into a tiny cold anteroom where a woman stood staring at a small table. While I watched she lifted a white cover and peered underneath at an emaciated baby with sightless eyes. Then she carefully replaced the cloth. Sister explained that the baby, only eight months old, had just died. The mother stood as still as though she were carved from stone.

Since the Feed-A-Family program of the NCCW could only help a small fraction of Korea's needy, it was decided to concentrate on a few specific programs. One of these was the anti-tuberculosis drive conducted by the Maryknoll Sisters' clinic. The Sisters chose several hundred families afflicted with T.B., and arranged regular home visits, regular courses of drugs, and vastly increased nutrition. Sister Mary Augusta, the American Sister in charge of the clinic, sent us some pictures and apprised us of the program's progress.

The Maryknoll Sisters carried on their literally back-breaking work for the T.B. sufferers. They continued the home visits for all advanced cases, and made regular checks on the progress of each patient.

In 1958 the Maryknoll Sisters opened a clinic in Chung Pyung, in the central part of Korea. There, too, Sister Mary Augusta told us of three-month old babies dying of starvation. Her report asked the question, "Why were these children in this condition? Because many hundreds are still being fed only rice water. Why, in a country where babies are traditionally breast fed with the nutritious milk God provided for mothers—why did these mothers not have milk for their infants? We saw and examined the babies as well as the mothers and realized that extreme malnutrition, vitamin deficiency, and diseases, chief among them tuberculosis, were the causes."

Sister Augusta's report continued, "At first, the women were reluctant in coming, and we were amazed to find that only five, ten, or fifteen could be persuaded to take advantage of the program. Then the first pre-natal patient delivered a healthy—and even fat—BOY, and the women began to flock to us. They thought our vitamins would produce not only fat babies, but, wonder of wonders, male infants to bring honor to the family. . . . Proper diet is almost an impossibility for many of our patients who live on barley and rice—and vegetables if they have them. We supply all the milk and vitamins. . . ."

Sister Carol, who had helped administer the Feed-A-Family program from their clinic in Pusan, was made director of the clinic in Chung Pyung and the NCCW funds were sent to her for her most needy families.

On a visit to our office in New York made shortly after she returned from Korea, Sister Carol told us of one of the mothers who had been enrolled for regular Feed-A-Family programs. "We called her Mrs. Bower," she said. "Her name was not as easy as that, but she bowed so correctly and so frequently to everyone in the clinic that the name attached itself to her. Mrs. Bower's husband had tuberculosis. We told her that in addition to vegetables and grains, her husband would have to have meat or fish now and then if he was to get better. The next time she came to the clinic she told us that good fortune was with her. A large dog had been killed on the road in front of her hut. She dashed out in time to put a claim on the body of the dog. However, three other families had been equally quick to move. (Dog meat is considered a great treat in Korea.) They all claimed their share of the dog. So they divided the dog between them. Mrs. Bower got the hindquarters, and she gratefully explained to us how she had boiled the dog and served it with rice."

In Korea, as elsewhere, the Feed-A-Family program changed gradually into a program of rehabilitation and self-help. The groups of refugees from the North, scattered in the countryside around Pusan, needed regular distribution of food, clothing and medicines merely to stay alive. Their crops were limited by the dryness of soil and the women had to carry the water for every household need from an open well.

Such water was most often polluted and was the cause of epidemics of dysentery and internal parasites.

A young Catholic Relief Services representative, Mr. John Donohue, wrote to Catholic Relief Services suggesting a very simple solution. Korean villagers, would, if they were given some initial help, cooperate in constructing protected wells, washing centers and latrines. The new wells would be protected from pollution by their depth and by cement walls. Deeper wells, however, needed a source of power to provide a constant water supply. The cheapest source of power in the world is the wind, and the simplest way of harnessing it, the windmill. The money needed to purchase the windmill, cement and a few other basic items was about one thousand dollars.

Feed-A-Family grants went to two refugee villages near Pusan, and soon windmills were whirling to help pump water for village needs. A short time after, we received pictures of Korean women washing their clothes at the spotless washing center, and proudly surveying a new communal water faucet that would give them and their families unpolluted water.

But the pockets of need that were met could not hide the lasting unmet needs of a gutted peninsula. There were signs—dread, unmistakable signs—that the years of violence, unrelieved want, homelessness, and above all, hopelessness, were taking their toll. From all over Korea came accounts of family suicide. The newspapers were full of what happened to family after family. Parents set a date for the whole family to escape together. There would be a final meal, leavened by poison, and then there was no cold, trapped tomorrow to face.

The dark drama of family suicide reached the headquarters

of Catholic Relief Services in two ways. A young Korean priest, Father Pak, on a mission for the Catholic Medical Center of Seoul, told us that he had just annexed a suicide prevention clinic to this Center. It was to be open around the clock to help give hope to despondent people contemplating taking their lives, and to people in the custody of the police after unsuccessful suicide attempts.

"Our people need help, yes," he told us, "but more they need hope. Our poor Koreans have suffered for so many years, and are still suffering. We must not judge them. We must love them."

Just about the same time, an SOS came to Mr. James J. Norris, Executive Assistant to Bishop Swanstrom, from a despairing father in Seoul. He had read in a Seoul newspaper of Mr. Norris' dramatic appeal before the bishops of the world at the Vatican Council for a stronger attack on world poverty. The writer explained that he could find no way out of his misery and no way to help his two children to a better life. He was in the hands of moneylenders and could not meet the back-breaking interest payments imposed on him. Despite broken English, his message was clear: "If you abandon me to nothing at all, we will decide on family's suicide. It will happen, and then you will see newspaper description widely. Esteemed friend, Mr. Norris, help me. Please. I hope . . . HOPE."

In responding to the needs of the suicide prevention clinic and of individual families with Feed-A-Family aid, we realized the crucial importance of hope in the lives of brokenhearted and broken-spirited Koreans. This realization made even more poignant our appreciation of a book by a Korean writer on the Calvary of his people. The central character of the novel, *The Martyred,* is a Christian minister who has lost faith in the eternal life, in the tenets of his church, but still preaches Christian hope to people whose lives have been shattered, blasted into a searing agony. He explains why he still preaches Christian hope: "I saw how despair paralyzed their spirits, how it snared them into the dark prison of their weary lives. The village had been bombed, shelled, sacked and nearly razed to the ground twice in the three months . . . Their young had been lost in the war, their daughters, sisters, wives, mothers had been raped; nothing to eat, nothing to cure their sickness—a hell on earth. I saw how men can come to be beasts without hope, how men can come to be like savages without the promise, yes, the illusion of eternal hope. Men cannot endure their sufferings without hope, without the promise of justice, if not here and now—and there is none—then somewhere else, in heaven . . ."†

Austria

A sudden and heartbreaking challenge to the Feed-A-Family program in Austria was occasioned by the flight of nearly two hundred thousand Hungarian refugees in late 1956, after the brutal repression of the Hungarian uprising. The Reverend Fabian Flynn, Director of the Catholic Relief Services Mission in Austria, wrote us about the Hungarian exodus.

"In the main," he wrote, "this is a great family flight—a family exodus. These people came not only from Budapest but from scores of towns, especially those near us at the Austrian border.

"It was a Sunday, when they heard that the Soviet Army had returned to Budapest with thousands of tanks. Whole

† Richard Kim, *The Martyred*, George Braziller, Inc., 1964. By permission of the publishers.

families walked out of their homes, closed the doors, and never went back again. They carried little or nothing with them so that they would be sure to reach the border before the marching soldiers.

"In no time at all, our Austrian camps, even the barracks that used to house the Russian soldiers, were filled. We went to visit these people in their obscenely crowded barracks. They were sitting on straw, tired and wet from having walked the snowy cold roads of November. They were in a strange land without money, and without an inkling of what their future would hold. It was then that the NCCW funds that were cabled to me were a godsend. We called them Help-A-Family funds because we could not make up food packages. We gave each needy family the money they needed to buy milk for the children and even a change of clothing. Every relief agency in Austria was mobilized to help these people. But there was never enough of the precise thing that they needed—especially clothing for the littlest ones."

Many families had to settle in the makeshift camps until missing members were located or until complicated immigration processing was completed. Father Flynn became head of a vastly augmented staff which had been flown in from the Headquarters of Catholic Relief Services in New York City and from agency offices in Germany, France and Sweden. The data needed before a visa was granted was considerable, and at this point the help of voluntary agency personnel was indispensable.

Staff members were fanned out through the main camp areas. A special team was on duty in Salzburg to service Camp Roeder where the Hungarians were readied for immigration to the United States. It was during the waiting period that nerves, tightened in the struggle against tyranny, became unstrung. During those grim, slack, uncertain months that followed the whirlwind of the Budapest rebellion and mass exodus, families needed extra assurance of love, of the concern of their fellows. Through the Feed-A-Family donations at his disposal, Father Flynn was able to see that the most anguished families received evidence of concern for their plight.

One letter from a camp in Austria read:

"You dear good people, your international help demonstrated to the whole world how happily we human beings could live, if only those people with charity in their hearts would exercise their power to lead.

"We will never forget you, who bring your suffering fellow-creatures the best gift of all—peace."

Latin America

When Catholic Relief Services inaugurated its feeding and medical aid program for the countries of Latin America, it was responding to the appeals of bishops, welfare leaders and of His Holiness Pope John XXIII, who gave the Church of North America a special responsibility in supporting the Latin American Church.

The almost immediate effect of the presence of personnel, funds and supplies from Catholic Relief Services was the growth and strengthening of local welfare agencies. Where an over-all Catholic Charities agency did not yet exist, its formation was speeded up. To Latin America, Bishop Edward E. Swanstrom sent Monsignor Alfred E. Schneider, who had directed the Catholic Relief Services aid program in post-war Germany, in India, Pakistan and Vietnam.

Monsignor Schneider's reports always emphasized the strange paradoxes of life in Latin America. From the Amazon's Mato Grosso, he wrote: "Near naked natives who have never seen a car in their trackless jungle, can recognize the very latest jet and propeller planes as they fly over their heads." In the cities the ultimate in luxury coexisted with unspeakable misery. The word *favela* appeared in his reports from Brazil, *barrio* in reports from Colombia, and *callampas* in those from Chile. They all referred to the same phenomenon—the massive mushrooming of slums that ringed Latin America's cities.

He wrote of Rio de Janeiro: "We have hundreds of thousands of people living in the *favelas* here. Some say over six hundred thousand. I live on the outskirts of town and the people have built their shacks on a steep hill which rises almost straight above me. There is no room for expansion because the city is ringed by steep hills. And yet they keep on coming.

"The people who cling to the peripheries of Rio, of such capitals as Bogota, Colombia, and Santiago, Chile, are an immense rural proletariat. Just think of nearly half a million people squatting around Bogota and four hundred thousand around Santiago. They still have a rural mentality. It will take them a long time to catch up with the skills and the manner of thinking that goes with city life.

"Meanwhile, though their lot looks to us pretty bleak, life on the edge of a city has some hope in it. They are not going to go back to the existence of the landless worker in the wilds of Brazil or Colombia."

Msgr. Schneider felt that northeast Brazil was the crisis region of a continent in crisis, its cities the most dreadful, the most miserable. The province of Bahia, in the northeast, was known as the "hunger province." It was also a province of thirst. A searing drought had put the final touch of tragedy to an outworn landholding system that had already reduced the peasants to a life of ignorance and need. Absentee landlords out of touch with the problems of the land, spent much of their time in the capitals of South America and Europe. The profits which might have been ploughed back into the land in fertilizers and irrigation systems were regularly poured out for good living far from the scene of the peasants' sweat and unremitting work. When the drought descended on Bahia the minimal life of the landworker became impossible. His tiny income from his work on the landed estates could no longer be eked out by the produce of his own garden. The region became one of *miseria morte*. Infants died of simple dehydration.

Families, in despair, left the barren country for the lush sea coast. One of the meccas they looked to was Salvador, capital of Bahia, and the first Brazilian town settled by the Portuguese in the sixteenth century. It is a town of great beauty, with a splendid cathedral and many marvelous shrines.

Awaiting the travelers in Salvador was Sister Dulce, who was always ready to receive famished people in a hostel that turned no one away. This frail nun was a native of Salvador and a member of the Brazil-founded congregation, the Missionary Sisters of the Immaculate Conception, which was started in 1910 by a German bishop in the city of Santarem. The first Sisters had come from Germany, but the order had taken root and in fifty years had over three hundred and fifty houses throughout Brazil.

The main work of this order was education. Sister Dulce had been a teacher, but was gradually drawn into social work for laborers and for the poor. Eventually, social work replaced teaching as her vocation. Her order supported her and gave her funds and a core of Sisters to work with her. The

Bahianos who had fled death in the thirsty land were dying on the dusty streets of Salvador. The hundreds of thousands who had been hurt by the drought were called the *"flagelados,"* the "beaten" generation—wherever they turned for help, they were beaten back and beaten down. By great effort, Sister Dulce established a large hostel, the *Albergue Santo Antonio.* Here the homeless families who had roamed the parched earth looking for a chance to live like human beings could rest for the night. They could be fed, and if ill, they would get first aid.

Monsignor Schneider, on one of his first visits to New York, urged that funds from the NCCW be allotted to the work of Sister Dulce. At this time, a medical and feeding project had already been set up by our agency in northeast Brazil, and a full time staff worker, Mr. John Wolf, was assigned to the area.

"Sister Dulce's work is very close to that of Mother Teresa in India," said Monsignor Schneider. "Can I give her a higher recommendation than that? She is in a situation not very different from Calcutta. People are at death's door when they come to her. Whole families come in from the hinterland. She tries to rehabilitate them. Tens of thousands squat in Salvador. They build their huts above the garbage dumps. This would be a perfect place for the NCCW Feed-A-Family program."

John Wolf's report underlined the urgent necessity for speedy action. He told of homes built on stilts on land filled in not by the city fathers, but by the accretion of city refuse. "The slums of Salvador," wrote Mr. Wolf, "are known as *'alagados.'* One of the plans of Irma Dulce is to build a school for the people of the *alagados.* These unfortunate people have built their tattered little havens on stilts on the swamp and tideland, foul-smelling holes with no sanitation, no clean water, and of course no streets. The sidewalks are on stilts made of old rotten boards laid in no particular pattern creating a very dangerous situation for less agile people to get around.

"We found this area inhabited by over 100,000 people, most with no employment, forced to make their livelihood by scrounging, stealing and begging. Only one doctor serves this whole area and he only comes twice each week for two hours. His facilities are: his small bag of emergency tools and an office or clinic as they call it about the size of a closet."

To help such families, through the hands of Sister Dulce, considerable Feed-A-Family funds were sent through the Brazil office of Catholic Relief Services. A Madonna Plan grant was added so that besides individual help, better medical service would reach the *alagados,* especially the mothers and the starving children.

The NCCW had been helping Sister Dulce for over a year, when they had the chance to meet her in person and hear from her own lips the needs of her people. The Biennial National Convention of NCCW was being held in Detroit, and through Catholic Relief Services, she was brought to the United States. The agency, which could in no way meet the dreadful needs of northeast Brazil, was hopeful that her presence would focus attention on the urgency of the situation and attract greater aid.

Before going to Detroit, Sister Dulce went to Washington where she conferred with the administrators of the Food for Peace Program of the Alliance for Progress and of the Organization of American States. Then she flew to Detroit and spoke at the Foreign Relief Workshop of the 32nd Convention of NCCW.

Following Sister's revealing talk was a film, "The Necessities of Life," which pictured the *alagados* of Salvador, the
homeless boys, the families arriving at the *Albergue Santo Antonio*. The sight of children walking over improvised clap-
board pathways raised on stilts to reach their bird-cage
homes, the whole scene reflected in the slimy water beneath,
made a tremendous impact on the women present.

Sister Dulce's talk had emphasized that the disorganization
of life in Brazil had broken family ties and left young children roaming the streets like little animals. She spoke of the
youngsters in these words: "We call these bands of boys 'The
Captains of the Sands.' They can be any age, from tiny
youngsters of five up to teenagers. Some of them do not remember ever being with their families. They do not know
even if they were ever given a name.

"What names do they have? They bear only the names
their companions have given them. Did you ever hear of a
boy being called 'Thing'? Yes, just 'Thing.' The word is
coisa in Portuguese, and that is what the boys in his pack
called him. Others answer to the names 'Rubber Lips,' 'Vam-
pire,' 'Burned Foot'—any descriptive word that a young person would think up. If they were ever christened, they do not
know it. They can only keep alive because they have learned
to steal cleverly, and lie. . . .

"When they see that I never punish them, that I never
turn them over to the police, they change. Believe me, they
are intelligent—even though they cannot read or write. They
all want to become mechanics—and some are already working
at jobs we have found for them. We need much help so that
someone called 'Thing' can be a man, a good man."

Through her attendance at the Detroit convention, Sister
Dulce served as a focus of attention on the continent of

South America, so pregnant with hope or threat for the future of the Western Hemisphere and for the world. One of the greatest dangers lies in the evil that could result if its most threatened families are not helped to find some place in society. The ways are many, including a reformed land-managing system, a return of the Christian teaching on property, and a basic charity that would reach out to pluck them from utter disaster.

One of those closest to the renewal of Latin America is Monsignor Joseph Gremillion, Director of the Socio-Economic Development Department of Catholic Relief Services-N.C.W.C. Spending much of his time in Latin America, and working to channel aid to any green sprout of self-help activity, Monsignor Gremillion came to an important conclusion regarding the Church in the Southern Hemisphere.

"The Church as a whole," he stated, "is no longer to be identified with the landed aristocracy, with the political oligarchy, and the oppressive status quo. Bishops, priests and lay leaders provide the new ferment for institutional reform. A network of social organizations including many types of co-operatives are 'putting flesh' on the concepts of social reform. We are clearly moving toward what we can call an incarnational Christianity in Latin America." In a small and individualized way, the Feed-A-Family program was part of a larger movement of 'putting flesh' on the Christian concept of charity.

In the fifteenth year of its existence, this family aid program was operating small projects in six Latin American countries.

In Venezuela, an energetic priest, Father Quinto A. Della Bianca, used Feed-A-Family funds in a plan similar to that of

Sister Dulce. In his vast parish of 80,000 he found women with the desire to work, but no available jobs. For one he purchased a kerosene iron so that she could support her seven children. For another he purchased an oven, for still another a wash tub and an ironing board. These women were then ready to turn out work that helped pay the grocery bill. In the *callampas* of Santiago, Chile, Feed-A-Family funds helped to move destitute families from wooden shacks to simple, but permanent homes. A local women's agency called 'Culture and Work' helped supply curtains, bed covers, sheets and mattresses, so that the family could start their new life with dignity.

Feed-A-Family aid is ready for emergencies as they arise. In a decade and a half, direct help has been supplied to families in Korea, Hong Kong, Vietnam, Thailand, India, Pakistan, Turkey, Lebanon, Austria, Italy, Berlin and West Germany. Through this program, the NCCW tried to live up to the blessing of Pope John XXIII:

. . . through your 'Feed-A-Family' program you are reaching out to aid some of the poorest families in foreign countries, especially those refugees who are shelterless, dispossessed and tempted to believe that they are abandoned by God and man. To these anguished families, your help has become an instrument to show forth God's loving providence towards the most defenseless and most victimized of His children.

6

To brighten their night of exile—
services by and for refugees

Man and beast

Cecelia was a Polish girl in her middle twenties who came
through our New York headquarters as a Displaced Person.
Three years before, she had barely escaped with her life from
Poland, in a flight that took her through Spain and Portugal,
and finally, to the United States. Her crime: she had saved
the children of a Jewish family for whom she worked. After
arranging their escape over the trails of the Pyrenees, she
became ill and had to wait behind in occupied France until
she was well enough to walk.

We talked about her flight and the fate of the many who
did not succeed in escaping from Fortress Europe. We discussed the millions who had been trapped in the net and sent
to the concentration camps where they were used in slave
detachments, or experimented upon like animals in a laboratory, or liquidated with unspeakable cruelty.

As Cecelia talked emotionally of the Nazi regime, I began
to see that those of us who had not undergone actual persecu-

tion still made use of outworn expressions and concepts. Even *homo lupus homini,* "man, the wolf to man," could not express the cruelty and terror those hunted Europeans had experienced.

"Beasts are gentle compared with man," she exclaimed. "When beasts hunt, it is for food. When they kill, it is only as much as they need to eat. A beast kills an enemy that threatens to take his mate, or to destroy him; he uses his own claws, his own teeth—whatever weapons go with his body. When a man tracks down someone he considers an enemy he is a million times more evil, a million times more terrifying, a million times more cruel. It is cruelty with no limits. He can call on the powers of nature and science to help him kill hundreds of thousands of people in one city. Most of them are not even his enemies—they can be children, the simpleminded, the insane, the sick. He kills them all."

The woman who consumed the Iron Curtain

After the Second World War, when the European continent began to break apart into hermetically sealed compartments, there was no name for the artificial and arbitrary barrier that was being established between East and West. As the Soviet Union refused to free the areas that its troops had "liberated," it became clear that an ideological, and, later, an actual wall, was being erected from Stettin, Poland, to Trieste. When Winston Churchill referred to this wall as the "Iron Curtain," the name caught the imagination of the world.

The Iron Curtain, cutting through the heart of Germany, claimed for its dark side the whole of Eastern Europe. Across this barricade came waves of refugees, all seeking to reach the brighter world that promised political and religious freedom.

The first to reach the West were the Displaced Persons, a
million and a half East Europeans who refused to return to
their newly-enslaved nations after World War II. Following
this group were the Expellees, German citizens or people of
Germanic ethnic origin, who were driven out of their homes
in Eastern Europe and in the sections of Germany ceded to
the U.S.S.R. and Poland. Third in time came the Escapees,
hundreds of thousands of Czechs, Poles, Rumanians, Hungarians, Yugoslavs and other nationals, who crossed the Iron
Curtain at the risk of their lives in the years following World
War II. A parallel movement was that of the three million
refugees from East Germany who fled to the West over a
period of fifteen years. The fifth group of East European
refugees comprised the Hungarians who breached the Iron
Curtain after the Soviet suppression of their uprising in November 1956.

For all of these groups the Foreign Relief Committee of
the NCCW had some program of aid which supplemented
the Catholic Relief Services programs. Even though their
contribution was necessarily limited, American Catholic
women never weakened in their aim to be, in the poet's
words, the "fingers of the Mystical Body," ministering to a
wounded humanity. The special help extended to Expellee
priests, and to newly arrived Hungarians is described in other
chapters.

Perhaps the most appreciated help was the continuous collection of good wearable garments by the affiliates of the
NCCW. The annual Lenten appeal of the Catholic Bishops
Relief Fund brought the needs of the homeless and hungry to
the attention of the United States. For one week, local radio

and television stations would help tell the story of people-to-people help under Catholic auspices. Bishop Edward E. Swanstrom's Campaign Director, Mr. Edward E. Kinney, supervised the preparation of the radio, television and parish promotional materials, and on the final Sunday of the campaign the factual material gathered and presented by Mr. Kinney was incorporated into parish sermons across the country.

Throughout Lent youngsters in parochial schools were reminded of children in foreign countries who lacked all the things they took for granted. Their teachers were given handbooks of the most outstanding problems prepared by the Commission of Citizenship of the Catholic University of America and made use of these in lessons throughout the day. In their classrooms a Calendar of Charity showed by pictures and text how gifts to the Catholic Bishops Relief Fund helped the poor throughout the world.

Catholic women, by contrast, were involved in the needs of the human family throughout the year. Through the pages of the NCCW magazine, "Monthly Message," later called "Word," the various programs of the committee were regularly presented. Issues of "The Works of Peace" and letters were sent out at regular intervals to Diocesan Presidents and Foreign Relief Chairmen in every part of the U.S. Through these methods women were continually mindful of the most victimized, the most humiliated of humanity, especially the refugees. From this awareness came the sewing groups who made new garments or mended old ones, and regularly sent shipments of finished clothing to Catholic Relief Services' warehouse in New York. During the Thanksgiving Clothing Campaign, women at the warehouse sorted and assembled the combined parish donations of wearable clothing with un-abated energy.

And so it happened that time and time again, a refugee on crossing the Iron Curtain would find needed clothing await-ing him at the office of Catholic Relief Services.

"We called it the 'Catholic Clothing' in the camp" (a camp for Escapees from Eastern Europe), said a woman from Prague. "It was for everybody, even for people without any religion, and that was good. We were all refugees, and I was glad that no person was turned away. . . . In that day I owned nothing in the world—my husband and my baby and I were together at last, but without even a change of clothes, except what N.C.W.C. gave to us."

I met the woman who told me this at a meeting of the Officers and National Chairmen of the NCCW in Washing-ton, D.C., in April 1961. She was Mrs. Charles Vachal from Prague, Czechoslovakia, one of the nearly three hundred thousand refugees who had come to the United States under the sponsorship of our agency. Plunging into community and church work, she became a leader of the Portland Archdioce-san Council of Catholic Women. She was then given a na-tional post, Vice-Chairman of the Civil Defense Committee, and in this capacity took part in the Leadership Institute of NCCW in Washington. Mrs. Vachal has since been made National Chairman of the Civil Defense Committee.

A natural leader, gifted with presence and a fine way of speaking, Giny Vachal told us a story that made her a symbol of the millions of people who had crossed the Iron Curtain after World War II. Many details were memorable, but unique and unforgettable was the fact that she publicly ate the Iron Curtain at a ceremony in which her family and friends participated.

She told us of the flight across the German border from Prague, taking with her only her wedding pictures and pills to put their twenty-two month old child to sleep with, of the time she, her husband and their son Edward had spent in refugee camps, and of their eventual arrival in the United States. "Then, to make the long, long story short—my husband is now the manager of a sawmill. The happiest day is when we became American citizens. We sent out invitations with the American flag. We put 'Former Residence Prague, Czechoslovakia' and 'Present Residence Waldport, Oregon.'

"After ten years in America, we must really celebrate. We have our own house. We send out invitations to the Open House. The sheriff came to the party, the State Senator, and also the engineer of the ship General McRay. He flew from San Francisco. At the Open House we had a big crowd. Nearly eighty signed in our guest book. Ten years in the United States, ten years of freedom. We have the highest honor of being Americans.

"We have a big cake. I want on that cake the Statue of Liberty. But the cake should show clearly what we are celebrating, so we put the Iron Curtain on the cake. From behind the Iron Curtain to the Land of Liberty.

"Everybody stands and looks at the cake. We take pictures of it. The first time the Iron Curtain is on a cake. Everybody smiles and I put the knife first in the Iron Curtain. I gave a piece to our State Senator and I say 'Have a piece of the Iron Curtain. Let's start to eat it.'

"He says, 'All right, Giny, let's eat it up.'

"And we did."

While Giny Vachal had humor and a lightness of approach, she was a person of the deepest seriousness. Her sense of purpose was related to an almost mystical faith—a faith that shone through everything she said. In her public speeches on Civil Defense, she went to bedrock doctrine for her arguments. She had the lyrical love for America that is shared by many whose rights were once in jeopardy.

The Vachals were one of the many families from behind the Iron Curtain to receive emergency help from Catholic Relief Services and from NCCW on arrival in the free world. After a few years in the United States, her husband prospered so that he provided his family with a comfortable hilltop home. Giny christened this *Hora Maria,* Mary's Hill. She then could have slowed down and built her life around ease and forgetfulness. But she had seen too much to want to forget the evils and dangers of the world, and she put her knowledge at the service of her new countrymen. As soon as she could speak English she began, like so many other refugees helped by Catholic Relief Services, to make real and lasting contributions to her home community, to her Church, and to the national scene.

Giny Vachal serves as an example of the countless refugees who came through the experience of camp life in Europe to a knowledge of and participation in American life. In contrast to this journey were many American women who took the reverse route, choosing to leave their homes in order to learn about and even participate in the lives of the displaced in European camps.

Two such women are Mrs. J. Selby Spurck, Foreign Relief Chairman of NCCW for four years, and Mrs. Robert Angelo, a former NCCW President and Chairman for Immigration.

Catholic Relief Services helped Mrs. Spurck plan her trip to Europe, a trip which she made at her own expense, to become more closely acquainted with the misery of refugee camp life. One of the camps she visited in Germany was

Uelzen, near the Iron Curtain. Here East German refugees were given shelter while waiting a place in the free world. From this camp and the others she saw, Mrs. Spurck brought back stories and memories which would bring the tragic results of war closer to the NCCW with whom she shared her experiences.

Mrs. Spurck told the women one story of Uelzen that had particularly shaken her. "I decided to have a few pictures taken at Uelzen," she told them. "They would help me picture the agony of the refugees when I talked to groups far removed, thank God, from such agony. I asked the photographer to take a picture of the little lame boy coming toward us, hopping along with the aid of a single crutch. The boy shook his head. He explained that he wanted to have someone else in the picture also.

"We followed him to the barracks where he lived, and he led us to one of the cots, where a woman who looked to be in her forties was lying. We thought she must be his mother. He took her face gently in his hands and moved it towards us. Then he sat down and waited to be photographed. The woman said nothing, but smiled faintly. So we took the picture and said goodbye.

"We asked the camp chaplain about the little boy and his mother. He told us that the woman was not the mother. In fact, she was only about twenty-three years of age. She had survived the liberation of one of the towns of Eastern Germany. The Russian soldiers violated almost every woman in the town. She was violated innumerable times, and found that she had been infected with a venereal disease.

"She was in complete despair when she was ordered to go to Aue, to work in the uranium mines. In a last burst of courage, she took to the road to make her way to West Germany. Near one town she found a lame little boy making his way along with the aid of a crutch. He had been separated from relatives and was looking for shelter. You could say that everything had been taken from this girl, but one thing, her woman's heart.

"She endangered her own flight to take the boy with her. She managed to reach Uelzen, and there they were given shelter. There was no place for them to go. Medicines from America cured her of the infection, but despair closed in on her. The little boy would not be separated from her, the chaplain told us. While she lay in bed, he took her food, sat with her. He was returning the love that she showed to him on the road. She began to show signs of rousing, and the camp social worker said that she had a good chance of recovery."

Trieste

Mrs. Robert Angelo of York, Pennsylvania, volunteered for a life that has tied her to some of the most desolate refugee camps of Europe, and as this was being written had completed over a decade of service.

Margaret McGinnis Angelo was elected President of the NCCW during World War II. The mother of seven children, she yet took on the heavy task of President, and continued in office even after her eldest son was killed in action. After her term was finished, Mrs. Angelo accepted the post of National Chairman for the Committee on Immigration of NCCW. She studied the subject of refugees, wrote cogent articles for the NCCW publication, and gained firsthand experience with the refugees themselves. Her first self-imposed duty was to canvass the local area around her home for job opportunities for the new immigrants, and along with thousands of other women associated with NCCW, "beat the bushes" for jobs and for homes and apartments.

The possibilities they uncovered were passed on to the Diocesan Director for Resettlement in each Diocese. These "DD's," as we called them, were in constant touch with the Resettlement Division of Catholic Relief Services. Through the network of charity thrown over the forty-eight states by the National Catholic Resettlement Council, close to three hundred thousand Displaced Persons and refugees were given the first vital contact with the U.S.

The Diocesan Director of Resettlement was always a priest who took on the refugee service as a second—or perhaps third—job. He was often a Director of Catholic Charities, or in a welfare position in the diocese. Mrs. Angelo, the members of her committee throughout the country, and other affiliates of NCCW were often the eyes and ears, hands and feet, of the busy priests charged with the resettlement of DP's and refugees. During the period of the various laws allowing for the refugee entry, it was necessary to provide for individual or agency sponsorship of each refugee family. The sponsor had to show that there was a job and a place to live waiting for the refugee.

In 1950, after I had participated in the Convention of the Harrisburg Archdiocesan Council of Catholic Women, Mrs. Angelo took me around the area to visit some of the Displaced Persons she had helped find homes and jobs. We started out from the Angelo home where many of the refugees had stayed for a few days while awaiting their local placement. As we visited a restaurant to see how a Polish DP was working out with the Czech restaurateurs and a farm where a Ukrainian couple were the managers, I saw that Mrs. Angelo was mother-counsellor-teacher to the people she had helped. She was sympathetic in difficulties, but firm in insisting that they study English and make efforts to integrate into parish and community life.

When her term was over as Chairman of the NCCW Committee on Immigration, Mrs. Angelo wrote me a letter explaining that she and her husband had become so deeply involved in the work of aiding Displaced Persons that she wondered if they could not continue aiding them. Mr. Angelo, she wrote, was considering retiring from his real estate and insurance business. They both felt that there was no better way to pass their remaining years than in service to the displaced and homeless. The next sentence made me pause: "We are willing and ready to go overseas, to wherever the need now is."

I passed on the Angelos' offer to the Director of our agency, Bishop (at that time Monsignor) Swanstrom. At his suggestion, the letter was turned over to the Right Reverend Monsignor Joseph J. Harnett, who had just returned from Europe and knew what personnel needs had developed. Monsignor Harnett, who had directed refugee and relief programs in France and Austria, was then tackling the problem of Trieste. The city, part of a Free Territory whose status was challenged by Italy and Yugoslavia, was situated at a very strategic point, the lower tie of the Iron Curtain.

Monsignor Harnett read the offer. "Mr. and Mrs. Angelo may be just the people we need," he said. "You know what is happening in Trieste. It is chock full of people from Venezia Giulia—probably a hundred thousand or more of them in every nook and cranny. Remember the Silos warehouse down near the railroad station—it is still filled with refugees from Istria."

I had seen the Silos warehouse on my trip to Trieste in

1947—a classic example of a refugee camp whose separate living cubicles were formed by hanging blankets and newspaper partitions. I had visited the four camps for Middle and East European escapees—Opacina, the Jesuiti, an old monastery, and San Sabba, a former concentration camp complete with small horrendous crematorium. An annex of San Sabba consisting of wooden barracks had been opened when the refugee influx was at its height.

"We still have about four thousand five hundred 'foreign' refugees in Trieste. We get the number down to four thousand, and in a few weeks of border-crossing, it's up to the old figure again. Every place is taken. We have a microcosm of the old Austro-Hungarian Empire in those camps—the Croats, Serbs, Slovenes, Hungarians, are all there—plus Bulgarians, Rumanians, Poles, Ukrainians and a few White Russians who quit Yugoslavia.

"We are just losing our two American staff from Trieste, our welfare officer and our business person for the U.S.E.P. cases."

The letters U.S.E.P. stood for United States Escapee Program, through which basic funds were channeled to worthy Iron Curtain escapees. Our agency was one of the American people-to-people organizations which disbursed these governmental funds along with other agency aid, to the escapees in question.

Desperately in need of assistants, Monsignor Harnett drove to York that very weekend. Mrs. Angelo was still anxious to donate her services as a full time volunteer for work in the camps. Mr. Angelo agreed to handle the business side—disbursing and reporting on the use of U.S.E.P. funds. He would accept a salary to cover basic living expenses.

Two weeks later, Mr. and Mrs. Robert Angelo were ready

to leave to take up work for Iron Curtain refugees. The day before they left, their two youngest daughters, Loretta and Margaret, decided they would go along with their parents for a short visit. A hurried dash to Washington, D.C., for passports and the whole family vacated the house together—and for keeps. Both girls, after seeing the situation in which their parents were making a contribution, decided to stay and make theirs also.

Mr. Angelo's work was at the office of Catholic Relief Services. Mrs. Angelo went every morning to one of the camps. The biggest single problem of those days was the presence of hundreds of unaccompanied young men, some only boys of fourteen, in the camps. They had come from Slovene villages just over the barrier from the Free Territory of Trieste, or from the Yugoslavian hinterland. The "dead end" boredom and chaos of camp life, which showed itself in the apathy of the older camp residents, expressed itself in wild mischief and delinquency among the young. Monsignor Harnett threw the seemingly hopeless problem to Mrs. Angelo as a challenge.

From her visits to the camps, Mrs. Angelo came to know the young men. She studied their outlook on life, their patterns of behavior. Her experience teaching grade school came to her aid. She went to a meeting of the welfare agencies with the first practical plan to attack the problem. She asked for official responsibility for the delinquents, and a barracks in the San Sabba camp for the sole use of unaccompanied young men. Both conditions were granted.

To start with she recruited a group of older DP's of the same nationalities as the teenage group. With their help, she organized a series of courses in the San Sabba barracks. Each man had a certain number of boys under his charge. He was to see that they turned up for classes, and he was to counsel them on their general pattern of conduct. The civic problems presented by unaccompanied youth showed a sudden drop. But final solutions are not reached in dramatic ways, and there were young men, especially the boys in their early teens, who were booked again and again for petty crime. Some of them were known as "wanderers." They would disappear from the camp, and reappear a week or ten days later after having crossed the frontier to take a look at their home villages and their families.

Monsignor Harnett said of Mrs. Angelo's work, "To her, no one was ever a 'case.' She had a face-to-face relationship with people always. She knew the names of the boys in short order. When they fell into the toils of the law, she was called for pre-trial hearings. She accepted responsibility for them and they were released in her custody."

The next group to which Monsignor Harnett asked Mrs. Angelo to direct her attention was that of the unaccompanied girls. Camp life was a moral trap for most of these unprotected young people. From a spiritual point of view Mrs. Angelo felt that new groundwork was needed. The girls were given the chance for a religious retreat in the country above Trieste. These retreats, voluntary for the girls, were so attractive in their setting, that they drew more and more girls. It was a combination vacation from the drab life of camp, and a chance to take stock of one's spiritual life. On a special plea from Mrs. Angelo, NCCW funds were forthcoming for the camp expenses involved.

Mrs. Angelo talked as a mother would; she told them they would never have a chance to emigrate unless they had some skill. The skill most needed to get a start overseas was that of homemaking—and that they could never learn in camp.

Catholic Relief Services rented a flat a few blocks away

from its Trieste office. Margaret Angelo brought the girls to the flat in groups of fifteen to thirty and took over the job of training them in domestic science. Cooking in a regular kitchen was a fabulous activity for these young women, who responded with enthusiasm to every chance to learn domestic science in the model apartment.

For years, the camps of jampacked Trieste could not send any of their residents for overseas migration. In 1950 and 1951, Migration Missions began to put the city on their itinerary. When the Australian Mission arrived, large groups of girls had been prepared by Mrs. Angelo both in English and in domestic science. A dinner at the apartment was an impressive proof of achievement; it contributed to what Trieste called "The First Australian Exodus." Fifty-eight refugee girls, snatched from the moral dangers and the emptiness of camp life, took off for Milan to board a special Milan-to-Sydney flight. Awaiting them were homes and jobs that had been screened by Australian governmental and voluntary agencies.

Mrs. Angelo, who was asked to talk on her work with the DP's at the 1958 Convention of the National Council of Catholic Women held at St. Louis in November 1958, told about the exodus. "That day, when they climbed aboard the plane, confident, dressed in good sweaters and skirts and smart sport coats supplied by NCCW, I could hardly remember the girls as I had first met them. They were bedraggled, withdrawn, suspicious. I thanked God for the chance to play a part in giving them what our children have as their heritage."

The services to unaccompanied girls reached a very happy point when the domestic science course was moved to a Trieste Catholic Center called the "Mater Dei." A long-term proposal of Mrs. Angelo came to fruition at the same time—a separate residence for the girls outside of camp confines. From that time on, the refugee girls lived in the "Mater Dei" home away from the demoralizing "mass living" of Trieste's depressing camps.

Mrs. Angelo presently turned her attentions to other groups as needy as the young women and young men, teaching English and literacy classes for near-illiterate old people. Monsignor Harnett told of the many times she would stand over a gnarled old woman, strange to a pencil, and urge her to practice writing her name. Her parties for the aged residents of the camps became a feature of Christmas in Trieste life. She regularly requested and received NCCW funds to provide a treat and a small useful gift for homeless old people who would otherwise be forgotten.

The tens of thousands of displaced Italians who were never able to move from the city benefited from the Feed-A-Family packages. A clinic which served the poorest of mothers and their children extended its services through a Madonna Plan grant of funds from the organization which Mrs. Angelo at one time led.

Ten years after the Angelo family took up their work in Trieste, the bishops of the United States approved a special prayer for refugees. This prayer seemed to describe the efforts of the Angelo family in entering a dark night of need with words and deeds of hope.

The prayer began: "Lord Jesus Christ, who chose to become an exile from Your heavenly home, grant that we, the exiled children of Eve, might not be banished forever from Your Father's face. You who as an infant in Your Mother's arms, fled into a strange land to escape the tyrant who sought Your life, we beg You to look with compassion upon the multitudes of men, women, and children in our own day who have been forced by other tyrants as cruel as Herod to seek refuge far from their homelands."

"Inspire in us," the prayer continued, "who have never suffered these misfortunes an ever-increasing spirit of charity . . . so that we may do more to brighten their night of exile."

7

Relief for Peace—
The foreign relief program of
the Catholic Daughters of America

Adopt-A-Family

The Catholic Daughters of America, with well over two
hundred thousand members, is one of the largest organizations of women affiliated with the National Council of Catholic Women. It is organized in units known as Courts in practically every state in the Union, as well as beyond the borders
of the United States, in Puerto Rico and the Panama Canal
Zone.

The Catholic Daughters gave strong support to every
aspect of the foreign relief program, and served as trailblazing pioneers in parts of it. Its Board of Directors called
the over-all foreign relief effort of the Catholic Daughters
Relief for Peace, echoing the words of Pope Pius XII who
commended American Catholic women for their overseas
charity in the following words: "The consolation afforded us
by your laudable achievements is all the greater because, as

we pointed out recently in our discourse to the Catholic women, by eliminating want, you become *messengers and promoters* of peace."

When the Children in Need collection of clothing was inaugurated in 1946, the Courts of the Catholic Daughters participated with notable generosity. A year later, their second overseas relief effort came into being at a meeting of the Board of Directors in Atlantic City. One of the items on the agenda was a fitting project to mark the forty-fifth anniversary of the founding of the organization. I was asked to talk on the developing programs of Catholic Relief Services and the part that Catholic women could play in these programs. I decided to relate some of the details of post-war living in Germany, Poland and Italy, as taken from the reports of our delegates in those countries.

In Germany, millions of dwellings had been destroyed in saturation and pattern bombing. Less visible but more horrifying was the number of families destroyed and broken by war and its aftermath—over fifteen million people caught up in a tidal wave of human agony. Herded into every form of available shelter in a defeated and occupied land, they had to scrounge for every morsel they put in their mouths. Plucked out of their homes in hamlets and towns of Eastern Europe, they found themselves among strangers, strangers too deeply sunk in their own world of care to have an ear for more misery.

The Allied Powers, the United States, Britain, France and the Soviet Union, considered the German Expellees a German problem. The German communities, already burdened by families whose breadwinners had been lost in the war, and by homes destroyed in bombing raids and shellings, were asked to deploy their resources to meet the needs of the expelled. *Burgomeisters* of thousands of communities commandeered every unused space, in attics, barns, half-destroyed hotels, to give the homeless some provisional shelter. Privacy had become an unheard of luxury.

Collective or racial guilt, a concept abhorrent to the Allies during the years of the war effort, had become, in victory, a principle of action; the expulsions were in accordance with the Potsdam Agreement of August 1946 signed by the major allies in Berlin, which put the Allies' stamp of moral approval on the mass expulsions conducted without regard to individual innocence. Children, above all, were the victims. After the terrors of war, they found the smallest things that had remained to give them a sense of security ripped away.

Berlin, the European capital most hideously torn apart by Allied air bombing raids, so that it no longer seemed a fit shelter for man, was receiving expelled wanderers every day. They came by road, by cattle train from points east. Shapelessly bundled up against the cold, they were seen around parks and zoo areas, gathering twigs and branches for tiny fires. Numbers of small children died during the first winter of peace. One report said that nearly all under three had died.

Daily bread was lacking; even wheat flour for the making of hosts was needed. In response to a cable from Catholic Relief Services in Berlin, a supply of the flour was flown into the battered city on a transport plane, enabling priests to distribute the bread of life to worshippers who were going through their own private Calvaries.

From Poland came the firsthand reports of Father Aloysius J. Wycislo, Assistant Director of Catholic Relief Services until he left the agency to become the Auxiliary Bishop of Chicago. Destruction had spared no part of the countryside, and no element of the population. On a country road, he met a small boy leading a cow by a rope. The priest stopped to talk to the lad, and noticed that the cow's tether was tied to the crook of the boy's elbow. As he looked more closely, he saw that the child had rough stumps where his hands should have been.

"Przewielebny ksieze, Holy Father, there were things that exploded in my father's field," said the child. "It was a mine that took my hands away."

The people of Poland, who had made a phenomenal recovery after the First World War, rebuilding hundreds of thousands of homes and devastated buildings, went to work on their country with the same relentless energy after the Second. But the first war brought reunited Poland into a new birth of freedom, while World War II saw the crucified country destroyed and again partitioned in favor of Russia.

In Italy, the poorest and least developed region, the *Mezzogiorno,* the lowest part of the boot, had been the most afflicted by a war action that started in Sicily and worked its terrible way up the length of the country. Even the hilltop villages of the bare southern mountains had not been spared. The towns of southern Italy were so denuded that even a heavy rain could carry off the few precious inches of top soil.

The members of the Supreme Directorate took a vote on a project to commemorate the Catholic Daughters' forty-fifth anniversary, and elected to link their Courts with the poor of West Germany, Poland and Italy.

Caritas in Germany and Poland, and the Pontifical Relief Commission of Italy supplied Catholic Relief Services with the names, addresses and descriptions of two thousand of the most destitute families in their countries. The German list stressed those expelled from their homes in the Sudetenland of Czechosolovakia, from Danzig, East Prussia and Silesia.

It was decided that the "adoption" of a family would entail sending regulation packages of food and clothing at least four times a year. What was sent in funds or special gifts over and above was optional. As it turned out, most sponsors regularly sent "extras," Christmas and Easter gifts to their overseas families.

Mrs. John V. Ballard, National Secretary of the Catholic Daughters, put in many hours organizing this project, assigning the European families to their benefactors in the United States. In most cases, the correspondence between the sponsor and the adopted family was conducted directly. Translation was accomplished through friendly contacts on both sides. Every week, often because of the pen of Mrs. Sara Varley McCarthy, Director of Public Relations, a few hundred needy families were linked with sponsors in the U.S. In a few months just about all of the two thousand families on the list had been given an American benefactor.

As time went on, the relationship between sponsor and European family often became that of friends. When the first terrible winters had passed and life in Europe began to return nearer to normal, members and Courts reported to the national office that letters from their European friends indicated that no more packages were necessary. But letters and contacts were continued for many years afterwards, and the memory of the charity did not fade.

One of the recipients of the food packages was a German woman struggling mightily to feed her family of five children. Her husband was having a difficult time returning to his profession after the interruption of the war years. In that lean time, when having enough to eat was a rare experience, the parents decided to adopt a sixth child—a boy fathered by an American Negro soldier. They had been approached by a desperate girl, not yet out of her teens, who was penniless, abandoned and pregnant.

After talking with the girl, who was considering an abortion, the woman finally saw that there was only one course to take: "This child will be a child of God like every other child born in Germany or in the world. Let the child be born. My husband and I will adopt it into our own family." They called their sixth child Donatus, after the saint whose name in Latin means "gift."

I met this courageous woman during a trip to Germany. I also met Donatus, a handsome boy whose mixed parentage gave him golden brown skin and beautiful black eyes. He was six then, already enrolled in school, happy and outgoing. When I asked what he wanted to be when he grew up, he smiled at me and replied, "Ein Pfarrer." "You notice," said his mother, "He has great spirit. He is not going to be just a priest. He intends to be Pastor."

Help-A-Priest

As soon as the "Adopt-A-Family" program was in full operation, the members of the Catholic Daughters of America learned of a new challenge to charity. When the massive expulsions into rump Germany had tapered off, it was found that there were over twenty-seven hundred priests among the Expellees. Their churches, schools, age-old cemeteries in the Sudetenland and Silesia were gone, since they had fallen on the far side of the Iron Curtain. But the priest, worn and exhausted as he might be, still had to be a tower of strength to his homeless flock. Just two years after the inauguration of the Adopt-A-Family plan the Catholic Daughters voted to set up the Help-A-Priest program and urged the Courts to sponsor an individual priest.

The sufferings of the war years were still not over for these men when, in the fall of 1949, I visited Schleswig-Holstein, an area which had doubled in population with the advent of Expellees from Danzig, East Prussia and northern Silesia. Many of these people were Catholics, and, with the priests who had accompanied them, they looked in vain for local Catholic parishes.

The Expellee priests often went straight to the local Evangelical rectories where they requested the pastor's permission for Catholic services in the only available church. In no case was their appeal refused, and so it came about that there was hardly an Evangelical church in all of Schleswig-Holstein which did not have one or more Catholic Masses every Sunday. But for the Expellees living in isolated camps, any corner of a barracks could serve, and the waiting rooms of railroad stations were regular centers for Sunday Mass.

In order to picture the condition of these priests the national headquarters of the Catholic Daughters circulated among the Courts a description written by a fellow priest, entitled "The Feet of the Apostles."

"I have before me," the account began, "a pen and ink drawing which has come to me from a corner of the battered continent of Europe. It is merely a picture of the feet of a man—feet covered with heavy but very worn shoes. It is clear that the shoes have been patched, but the left shoe is so badly worn that the toes come through. The man wearing the shoes evidently has no stockings on at all.

"The title of this picture of feet is *'Pedes Apostolorum,'* 'The Feet of the Apostles.' The little picture was drawn from life, and it represents the feet of those who tread in the steps of the Apostles of old. These feet are those of a homeless priest, who since the war, along with millions of men, women and children, has been expelled from a home place in the Eastern section of Europe into the hungry and destroyed area of Western Germany."

It was not long before the eight hundred neediest among the expellee priests, whose names and addresses we had supplied to the Catholic Daughters, were getting letters from unknown benefactors asking for the opportunity to aid the priest in his mission. Food, clothing, medicines, bicycles, motorcycles, funds began crossing to the remotest hamlets in West Germany.

An album was compiled of hundreds of letters from these priests—an album that was evidence of a deep spiritual reality. Reading those letters of gratitude gives not only a picture of the already forgotten nightmare of post-war need in Germany but also the growth of the "economic miracle." Outside aid coupled with phenomenal German energy and organization changed the face of the ravaged land. One by one, the uprooted priests wrote that they had become established in West Germany, that new churches had been built in the diaspora, and that their parishioners could meet their needs and the needs of the transplanted parishes.

Vietnam

The Tonkin Delta area of Vietnam and its heavily Catholic population fell to the north of the 17th Parallel and to the domination of the Communist regime of Ho Chi Minh, when the country was divided by the Geneva Truce Agreement of July 1954. The people now in North Vietnam faced the choice of remaining in their home villages or moving to an unknown future south of the 17th Parallel. The communist government offered them all sorts of economic betterment, but experience had taught them that freedom, especially religious freedom, could not exist north of the Parallel. For their faith, and the faith of their children, most Christians began their pilgrimage to the south during the three hundred day "grace" period after the signing of the Truce Agreement.

Again Catholic Relief Services supplied the documentation on each priest exiled in South Vietnam, and the Catholic Daughters, with the help of our office, acquainted the membership with the dimensions of the problem. One by one, the aged and infirm among these priests began to receive help through the intermediary of our Saigon office. Many of them had been weakened by torture and by periods spent in communist jails. It was for these priests especially that help was wanted. At the time, money was the only form of aid that could be supplied. Dollars would be changed into Vietnamese piastres at our Saigon office and delivered to the individual priests through the welfare network Monsignor Joseph J. Harnett had set up on the basis of parish and diocesan units of resettlement.

A member of our Saigon staff translated the letters the Catholic Daughters sent to the priests into Vietnamese. The letters of thanks, in turn were rendered into English before they were sent on to New York.

The lines of contact established by the Courts and individual members of the Catholic Daughters of America with priests half a world away continued for many years, in fact, well into the nineteen sixties. The letters that arrived mirrored the drama of life in Vietnam for communities in the United States. The letters that suddenly stopped coming brought the continuing agony and peril of Vietnamese life into American living rooms.

The latter happening was the case with Father Joseph

Minh who had been writing steadily to Court Santa Maria. He was pastor in the village of Kon Kela in the remote high plateau region of South Vietnam. When his letters suddenly ceased, the members of the Court were brought close to a common tragedy in Vietnam. The hammer of international communism was hurled unmercifully at the communities of South Vietnam from mountain fastnesses, from the shelter of the thick tiger-infested jungles, from across nearby borders. Simple people in struggling new communities were brutally murdered, lepers were thrown out of hospitals and the buildings gutted of all equipment; village leaders and priests were targets for the assassins. Father Minh was one of the victims.

Because of arthritis Father spent what proved to be the last four days of his life in the clinic founded by Dr. Patricia Smith in Kontum, the capital of the western mountain provinces. Dr. Smith, a young American woman, had volunteered to work for the Vietnamese in a cooperative effort between the Grail Lay Mission Group, the Bishop of Kontum and our agency.

On a visit to the United States, Dr. Smith met with Miss Mary C. Kanane, then National Secretary of the Catholic Daughters. They naturally began to speak of Father Minh.

"I warned Father Minh not to go back that day. He was in pain, and he could just barely walk," said Dr. Smith. "But it was a Saturday, and he wanted to say Mass for his village on Sunday. His cousin came to drive him up to the mountains. He never saw his villagers again. The jeep was ambushed by a band of communist guerrilla fighters. They swooped down from some mountain hideout. He was shot dead by the roadside. His cousin survived."

Mary Kanane's conversation with Dr. Patricia Smith led to a new program departure for the Catholic Daughters of America. After hearing the description of needs in the mountain provinces of Vietnam, it was decided that a Madonna Plan grant given by the Catholic Daughters would be channeled to Kontum to help with a midwifery course under the direction of Dr. Smith.

Dr. Pat was a colorful personality, a young American who, when her studies were finished, looked for a way to serve those cut off from medical help. Her first patients were in the mountains of Kentucky, but the blazing words of Elizabeth Reid of the Grail turned her mind to the needs of the Orient; and it was to the jungle mountains of Vietnam, to the tribes of the High Plateau, that she went with her compassion and her skills.

I saw the Bahnar tribes people during a stay in Vietnam. Primitive, small people who looked more like South Sea islanders than the Vietnamese of the coast, they wore almost no clothes. The men wore a breechcloth, the women wrapped themselves in a sarong-like garment which left the upper part of their bodies bare. Msgr. Harnett and I had visited the strange villages in the jungle clearings, small huts on stilts clustered about a community house, the "Long House," also on stilts. The elders of the Bahnar villages, whether Catholic or animist, received us with honor, giving us the VIP treatment which consisted of the gong orchestra, a triumphal decorated archway, and an array of gifts—bows and arrows, foods, the great jars of rice wine.

One village a few hours ride from Kontum stood out in my memory. Its population was composed of the outcasts of all the neighboring villages—lepers who were led out of the village confines when their disease became evident. They were usually led about a mile away from their home village where they were given a little hut to shelter them. From then on, they had to fend for themselves, slowly rotting away from the terrible, unchecked progress of the disease. A group of lepers from a large area came together in a bleak spot at the edge of the jungle and had formed their own village.

When we arrived towards evening, they were waiting for us with the gong orchestra, and a pathetic attempt at an arch of welcome covered with green branches plucked from the jungle. The hands which held the rods to strike the gongs had stumpy fingers, half eaten away. The feet of our welcomers were toeless. Some stared out of sightless eyes, others had bulbous and ravaged faces. They wore ragged striped blankets over their breechcloths and sarongs against the cold of the mountain evening. To make us feel at home, they stood before us and sang songs in the Bahnar tongue. The Christians among them sang a hymn and then bowed to us.

When Dr. Patricia Smith volunteered to work in Vietnam she was planning to live in Kontum. It happened that the little house reserved for her was not vacated in time for her arrival and shortly after, we received news that she was living in the village of lepers. A Daughter of Charity from France, Sister Marie Louise, was then living in the village giving daily care to the forgotten people. Dr. Smith decided to live there, too, learning the treatment of the disease, and learning the Bahnar language from the lips of her leper patients. For six months, her home was a hut just like the other villagers. She boiled her medical instruments in a large pot, stored her medicaments in a kerosene refrigerator, installed by Sister Marie Louise under the raised floor of her hut.

After hearing of Dr. Smith's experiences and achievements in Vietnam it was decided that the Catholic Daughters of America would make a grant of funds available through

Catholic Relief Services-N.C.W.C. for the first year of the midwifery course, and possibly for succeeding years.

Later, at our office, Dr. Pat introduced us to Miss Helen Perry, the registered nurse who would help her set up the course. Miss Perry had served as a Public Health Nurse and trained midwife in New Mexico, and knew the Orient through Red Cross work in Korea. She was anxious to put her varied nursing experiences to work.

Korea

The Catholic Daughters began their long involvement with Korea in June 1953, when South Korea was invaded by forces from the land north of the 38th Parallel.

As the "police action" in Korea enveloped more and more of the peninsula, the armies of sixteen nations became involved in the fighting. The stone buildings of cities and the thatched homes of villages were reduced to ashes by MIGs and jet bombers as the forces from North Korea pushed soldiers and civilians southward to the coast. The crush of millions of people in the perimeter around the southern port of Pusan made for dreadful homelessness and suffering.

Eventually, the trooplandings at Inchon in central Korea relieved the pressures on the southernmost part of the country. Then the terrible plight of Korean civilians began to be really known.

In the southwest, the inhabitants were reduced to actual starvation. Whatever food was ready for harvesting was snatched by guerrilla fighters still hiding in the remote areas. Bark disappeared off the trees, taken by the country people to be boiled and chewed.

In Mokpo, the port town of remote southwest Korea, Monsignor Harold Henry, an American Columban Father, served as Vicar Apostolic. On behalf of his starving people, Monsignor Henry sent a cry for help to Monsignor George Carroll, Catholic Relief Services Director for Korea. The appeal was answered immediately with the purchase of ten thousand dollars worth of rice from funds donated through all the affiliates of the National Council of Catholic Women. Monsignor Carroll asked if the women could not promise regular aid for the denuded area of Mokpo.

The Adopt-A-Family program which the Catholic Daughters had embarked on in 1947 had already passed its peak. Of the families aided in Europe more and more were writing that they no longer needed help. When the Catholic Daughters heard of the appeal of Monsignor Henry, they felt their membership was ready for the new challenge. It was still a family aid program, but there could not be the same direct contact there had been in the European program. The donors would give five dollars monthly for a Korean family, the funds to be placed in the hands of Monsignor Henry. Every month the funds went off to Korea through a bank transaction in New York. Never was a penny subtracted, misdirected or lost.

In the town of Mokpo itself, there was a special drama connected with the distribution of rice, a story told us by Monsignor Henry himself. He had to return to America, and was subsequently invited to talk at the National Convention of the Catholic Daughters of America held in Minneapolis in July 1955. As he stood in the hotel ballroom before two thousand women, he held out a plaque.

"This plaque comes to you, the Catholic Daughters of America, from the mayor of Mokpo. He thanks you for coming to the help of his people when they were helpless in the face of starvation and when they feared that they and their children would be forgotten by the world. As you did not forget them, they will never forget you."

"I would like to tell you a sidelight," continued Monsignor Henry. "I talked with the Mayor of Mokpo and with other Korean officials and told them that the food came from Catholic women in America and was meant for the poorest of the poor without distinction. We worked with them to locate the people nearest starvation and we set up our distribution points. In Mokpo, when the rice storehouse was filled, our Catholic people could be forgiven for expecting first call on Catholic charity.

"This was where we had to emphasize 'universal' as the true meaning of Catholic. We told our people that as they were not always the most needy, they would take their turn after the hungriest had been fed. They accepted this very well— for, mind you, everyone was hungry in those days. It was just a matter of degree.

"The Korean officials and the hungry of Mokpo were surprised beyond measure. I realized then that they had never taken me at my word. They helped give out the food to the neediest on the basis of need alone. The natural tendency in any community to favor some over others was overcome, partly because of our adamant stand in favor of the most helpless. One day a Korean official came to me and said wonderingly, 'Now we know that you were telling the truth after all. We saw you feed the neediest Koreans who were not Christian before you gave anything to the Christians.' Thank you for helping to relieve suffering in this poorest province of a poor and destroyed country."

Korea, still in desperate need, received the monthly donations of funds for the decade following the hostilities. During that period Monsignor Henry was consecrated Bishop and then Archbishop. His diocese is centered in Kwangju, and includes Mokpo and the greater part of southwest Korea. As Mokpo lacked medical facilities, he brought the Columban Sisters, trained as doctors and nurses, to set up a clinic and, later, a hospital. In time, most of the funds were channeled through the Sisters, who had to give extra food to their patients if they were to recover from their illnesses.

When Archbishop Henry found himself faced with another imminent need, he appealed directly to the Catholic Daughters of America, accompanying his plea with a dramatic photograph. An unpaved, dusty road, empty of people or vehicles, slashed through the center, with a group of children standing on one side of it. They were healthy well-dressed youngsters, smiling and waving their hands. On the other side of the road was a large group of men and women who were kneeling and looking intently at the children across the way. The picture was entitled "Visiting Day at Sorokdo."

Sorokdo was the large leper colony of southwest Korea. The children on the one side of the road had been born in the colony. They were the untainted children of the lepers who were kneeling on the other side. They had come to visit their parents. They could talk back and forth and keep in contact with each other, but the only safeguard was separation. The road down the middle of the photograph was a real barrier, an invisible wall.

These children had been given to the care of Archbishop Henry. He built a fine nursery and child care center and arranged for regular visits with the parents. Leprosy, a real scourge in Korea, increased during the Korean War. Treatment was suspended, infected people left the gutted leper colonies and spread the disease. One of the plans of the desperate administrators of the leprosariums was to sterilize every person committed to one of their institutions. There were many Christians in Sorokdo who objected to the operation, and Archbishop Henry vehemently supported the objections.

The reply came back to him that if he would take charge of all the children born to lepers, compulsory sterilization would not be enforced. But even untainted children develop the disease from day-to-day contact with infected parents—the only answer was a nursery, and in time, Archbishop Henry had one which held three hundred children. Separate housing had to be built as the children grew older. Austrian nurses came to take charge of the infants. Since there is no free school system in Korea funds were needed for the youngsters of school age. At this point Archbishop Henry appealed to the Catholic Daughters of America for help.

A leaflet was prepared showing some of Korea's helpless, and this and Archbishop Henry's appeal were studied at the 1962 Annual Meeting of the Catholic Daughters in Denver, Colorado. Miss Margaret J. Buckley, as Supreme Regent, and Miss Mary C. Kanane, as Relief for Peace Chairman, explained the plan for these children. The sponsor of an individual child would give ten dollars monthly for his or her complete support. The Archbishop himself would send a picture and description of the child who was being helped. Letters of thanks would go to the sponsors, not directly from the child, but from the Chancery of Archbishop Henry in Kwangju. This program was so well accepted that within a few months almost every child in Archbishop Henry's care had received a sponsor in the United States.

The new Relief for Peace chairman, Mrs. Manila Caprine, took over the time-consuming task of routing the hundreds of monthly contributions to the individual children in the Archdiocese of Kwangju. At the direction of Miss Margaret J. Buckley and the Board of Directors, the "Special Child Project" was expanded to embrace not only the untainted children of leper parents, but also children in Archbishop Henry's orphanages and children in poor families who, without outside help, would pass through childhood without any formal education.

In this "Special Child Project," and in their other programs of giving, the Catholic Daughters were fulfilling the teaching of His Holiness Pope John XXIII on the true meaning of peace. "The foundations of peace," said the Holy Father, "are nothing else than true justice, true love, and a generous willingness to give and to give oneself for one's brother."

8

Happiness and human anguish

"To contemplate the misery of another without turning away, that is beautiful," wrote Simone Weil, an exile from Europe during World War II.

To understand why so many American Catholic women did not flinch before the spectacle of the world's anguish, we can turn to the words of another woman, a Doctor of the Church and a saint, Teresa of Avila. "Christ," she said, "has no body now on earth but yours, no feet but yours. Yours are the eyes through which Christ's compassion is to look out on the world: yours are the feet with which he is to go about doing good. . . ."

Because they did what they could to look out on the world with Christ's compassion, women have accomplished the deeds related in this book. *The Works of Peace* cannot be merely a record of achievement; it must seek a deeper level, an enquiry into meanings.

From childhood, we are acquainted with the story of Lazarus and "a certain rich man who used to clothe himself in purple and fine linen, and who feasted every day in fine fashion." To identify with the Lazaruses of our world is our admission that we are all beggars before God. To choose to be close to the poor and suffering in time is to choose not to be separated from them in their eternity of peace.

A central question is how people can remain so conscious of pain and suffering, can become closely involved with the healing of pain and relief of suffering—and yet maintain an inner core of happiness. Certainly one weeps for the pain of others; certainly one feels with the pain of an Indian mother who tries to save her child from leprosy, of a girl maimed in spirit and body lying in the corner of a refugee camp like Uelzen. Natural compassion is simply "feeling with," but it is supernatural when one "feels with" those who suffer even though they are not known personally, because we are all one in Christ.

In all this weeping and "feeling with," where is happiness hiding? Here lies a paradox, one of the many of Christian life. We learn in the Beatitudes, "Blessed are the merciful, for they shall obtain mercy." The word "blessed" is the old translation, and takes our mind to the blessed hereafter when all good works will stand us in good stead. But both Greek and Latin come to our rescue, by giving the meaning of the first word of each Beatitude as "Happy." Since *beatus* in Latin and *makerios* in Greek stand for being happy in the here and now, it has been pointed out that the Beatitudes should be simply called the "Happytudes." They are, in fact, an eightfold path to happiness. We should be saying, "Happy are the peacemakers. . . . Happy are the merciful."

Pope Paul VI stressed that "in its essential manifestation Christian life is happiness," when he gave his first Easter message to the entire world. "Recall," said the Holy Father, "the program of life laid down by Christ in the Beatitudes. You will see that it is essentially positive . . . it is human. But it is more than human, for it is permeated by the vivifying and ineffable presence of the Spirit, the consoler, the spirit of Christ, who comforts and sustains it, and gives it the power to perform superior acts of believing, of hoping, of loving. . . . It enjoys happiness today in expectation of perfect happiness tomorrow."

Now we come back to compassion. This leads us to the works of mercy, and the works of mercy bring us peace of mind here and now, because we know that we have lessened the pain of a human being like ourselves, a human being who has been bearing an enormous cross. If we had refused to contemplate the misfortune of another, if we had blocked the love of God struggling to act through us, if we had turned away to face the little joys and pleasures we know so well, we would not have gained the present happiness—a happiness that is often almost palpable when we transcend ourselves to meet another's need. The "Happytudes" are a reminder that we do not find happiness by pursuing it, but that it comes to us as a side issue, a side product of something else—something good. The "happytude" most pertinent to *The Works of Peace* is one that was put to the test by millions of women in their study and efforts for overseas aid. By putting out their hand to the needy the women knew that they were meeting much more than the corporal necessities of the naked and the hungry—they were bringing consolation to those who had known God chiefly by his rod; hope to the many who had reason for despair.

The constancy of the women was supported by the messages to them from the Fathers of Christendom—messages quoted in this narrative—which stressed the supernatural basis of Christian compassion undergirding the natural springs of compassion.

One of the Moderators of the National Council of Catholic

Women, Monsignor Clarence D. White, drew up diagrams representing the whole scheme of the Christian life, to remind the women of their relationship to humanity. He drew a circle to represent the individual Christian, who is a witness of Christ. By Baptism and Confirmation one attains the character of a mature Christian in the Mystical Body of Christ. As he is the Way, the Truth and the Light, each of us becomes witness to the way, truth and life of Christ—the way of faith, the truth of Christ's revelation, and charity. "A Christian," said Monsignor White, "is sent to bring faith, truth and charity to 'others.' The 'others' are, first of all, the individual person, represented by another circle of the same size. Then comes the family of which we are a part, a larger circle. Next comes the community in which we live, a still larger circle. Finally a large englobing circle represents the world society of nations. The person can reach these larger circles through the lay apostolate."

Monsignor White put his thoughts on the apostolate in simple rock-like formation: "Prayer strengthens faith, the essential for personal responsibility and Christian formation. Study gives knowledge of truth, necessary for public morality and based on Christian principles. Action for others expresses charity, fundamental for human dignity." The work of the Foreign Relief Committee rested on the rock of 'prayer-study-action' in proceeding from the smallest circle to the largest encircling the world.

As I gave speeches to women's groups in most of our states, I was struck over and over again by the special power of the foreign relief program to coalesce into joint effort women of widely disparate views, national origins and levels of education. Of the many meetings and conventions I attended, one stands out in my memory because it gave me a new insight into the persistence of the women in their hard work for overseas aid. It was held in Salina, Kansas, in the heart of the rich wheat country of the Middle West. The homes that I visited were simple, quiet and comfortable. Life was about as peaceful as it could be anywhere; but the women of Salina showed, by the questions they asked and the donations they gave to Madonna Plan, that their own comfort did not shut out the thought of places where life is marked by upheaval and anguish. The last exercise of the convention was held in Salina's cathedral. As we approached, I was astounded to see that it rose out of the flat landscape like a glorified wheat elevator with a tall silo for a tower. In color it was a golden wheat tone. On the outside was a bas-relief representing the faithful carrying the fruits of the field and the work of their hands as a thank-offering to God. As the women took me around this striking example of American church architecture, I felt that their overseas charity might be seen in the same light, as a thank-offering for the peace and order of their lives.

It is tempting to describe many such meetings, and many women whose work was outstanding, but I will cite three examples of women from different areas of the country, of varying temperaments and backgrounds, but united in their constant work and sacrifice for voluntary overseas aid. Each of the three led lives that would have made it easy for them to retreat and insulate themselves from others' misfortunes. Each shows how in a time when the individual may feel helpless before need and threats of destruction, the zeal of one person can dispel apathy and spark commitment in others.

Mrs. Thomas H. Kenny, who wished to help make a better world for the suffering and a better world for her grandchildren to live in, was chairman of the Foreign Relief Committee of the Diocese of Brooklyn. While chairman, she gathered around her a core of workers from the Brooklyn Diocesan

Council of Catholic Women. Any woman's talents could be used. Even the aged were able to share in the program and contribute to the world community. For years one older woman knitted woolen squares which were sewn together to make quilts for T.B. victims in Korea.

At meetings and conventions of Catholic women, Mrs. Kenny hovered over the display of relief clothing, explaining where they would be used, and urging Brooklyn women to search through their closets for the garments that would replace the rags of a Chinese refugee in Macao or those of a family in the slums of Rio de Janeiro. Not only did the clothing flow in—no less than 100,000 garments yearly—but thousands of dollars were donated for all the Foreign Relief programs.

Gertrude Kenny explored every avenue in her personal and family life for possibilities of gifts. Through her husband's business associates, she learned that certain manufacturers often discarded, or sold for a fraction of their cost, large numbers of imperfect dresses and housecoats. The cotton housecoats would be perfect hospital wear for the poor in Asia. Mrs. Kenny informed the clothiers that their rejects would be gratefully received in many countries overseas and that Catholic Relief Services would be a channel for sending them to people in need. Happy to have found a reliable outlet, the manufacturers began to make regular gifts of dresses and housecoats with imperfections that were hardly noticeable to the naked eye. Mr. Kenny supplied the trucking to transport the clothing from the factories. When the gifts overflowed the basement of their home and their garage, a druggist in Queens made an empty store available as a depot to all who wished to contribute relief clothing.

An unbroken stream of slightly imperfect garments from manufacturers, as well as new and used garments collected in the Children-In-Need and Papal Storerooms Collections, flowed into the charity depot. It was open throughout the day, every day in the week. The clothing was regularly transported to the warehouse of Catholic Relief Services for baling and shipment overseas. Every year thousands of the poor and suffering in Latin America, Africa and Asia exchanged their rags for clothing which restored some human dignity to their lives—all this because of the tireless efforts of one zealous woman.

Another striking example of the works of mercy came from the City of Brotherly Love. Mrs. Sylvester Lowery of Philadelphia paid a visit to the office of Catholic Relief Services in the spring of 1947. She had undertaken the organization of a Children's Aid Committee under the sponsorship of Cardinal Dougherty of Philadelphia, and through this had collected considerable amounts of money for orphans and needy children in Europe.

Mrs. Lowery came to the headquarters of the bishops' overseas aid agency to find out if there was any special project which the women of Philadelphia could take on as their own responsibility. The Director of Catholic Relief Services, Monsignor Patrick A. O'Boyle (soon to become Archbishop of Washington, D.C.), explained that one unmet need was a great concern to him—that of the Carmelite convents in the war-ravaged areas of the world. The "Praying Church" was in real danger at a time when humanity was truly in need of prayer. The C.R.S. Director had received requests for all forms of aid; the cloistered sisters lacked everything, food, religious habits, even shelter in those communities hit by bombs.

As Mrs. Lowery belonged to the Adoration Society, she felt that she could interest her friends and fellow members in the special problems of the Carmelite Sisters overseas. She took some of the requests back to Philadelphia and reported that families were filling them with great enthusiasm. Children joined in a hunt for the small items that were difficult to obtain in post-war Europe—safety pins, buttons, toothpaste, soap. One appeal had particularly impressed the women. A nun had written from a destroyed European town to say that the Sisters were so weak from hunger, and their ragged habits such poor protection against the cold of the convent that they had been advised to remain in bed. The townspeople, who used to bring food and other gifts to the convent, were so desperately poor themselves that they could spare nothing.

Catholic Relief Services agreed to ship the donations to Europe and Asia provided they were packed for export in Philadelphia. This necessitated three things besides volunteers: a center in which to pack the food, habits and other gifts, a trucking service to the center, and heavy wooden crates which would withstand the rigors of port handling and loading. Mrs. Lowery soon found a center, a former stable on the grounds of the Academy of the Assumption in Ravenhill. The trucking was done by volunteers, and the committee collected funds to purchase the wooden crates.

An appeal went out to Philadelphia parishes, not only for the needs of the cloistered Sisters, but for the war stricken in the countries served by Catholic Relief Services. The response was so great that to keep the clothing from flooding the stables, it was necessary to have volunteers there seven days a week to pack and stencil the cases of relief goods. Thus began a regular five-day working week for a core of volunteers led by Mary Moran Lowery, who was later made Chairman of the Committee for Foreign Relief of the Archdiocese of Philadelphia, an affiliate of the NCCW.

At the Las Vegas Convention of the NCCW, Mrs. Lowery was asked to talk on her foreign relief work. She told us of some of the appeals her Committee had answered. From Manila there had come a plea for Communion hosts. 40,000 hosts were immediately flown out. Convents sent requests for host-baking machines; these were located and sent off. Flower and vegetable seeds were asked for, and were supplied for convent gardens in Europe. Sewing machines were sent to several cloistered convents. Prescription glasses were airmailed to teaching Sisters in Poland. The most bizarre request came from a convent in Austria—the nuns wanted a supply of "eyes" and "blond hair." They made small statues of the infant Christ and had run out of supplies. The "blond hair" was donated by a young girl who entered the Carmelite Convent in Philadelphia. A large box of eyes was sent as a gift from a doll hospital in the city. The Carmelites of Haifa, Israel, appealed for a washing machine. Funds were sent for its purchase. Sisters in Honduras and Salvador appealed for First Communion dresses for their pupils and thousands were packed and shipped out.

In meeting large and small requests, the Committee for Foreign Relief of the Philadelphia Archdiocese was so faithful that it became known as "the group that never said no." In seventeen years of activity its donations reached nearly seven million dollars in value.

A third instance brings us to a young mother of seven children, Mrs. O. E. Wolford, of Detroit, Michigan. Her special talents were speaking and writing, and she put these at the service of the NCCW. While serving as National Chairman of the Committee on Public Relations, she used her gifts to spread the story of overseas charity. She once phrased her concern for foreign relief in these clear and meaningful terms:

"A sickly, hungry child in Brazil," said Jane Wolford, "an Indian mother bowed under burdens beyond her strength, a Korean family so plagued with the terrors of poverty they seek the oblivion of death—but for the grace of God, these children of God could be myself or my family. Christ hung from a cross and died for them as well as for me. These illiterate, outcast poor are my brothers and sisters just as much as the people who kneel at Mass with me. How can I close my heart to them? I cannot. In fact, I do not feel I have the option to forget them once I know of them. I must promote their cause with the talents I have, within the framework of the channels I can use."

To see the needs of the family of man as clearly as the needs of one's own family is to look at the world with Christian eyes. Every act of putting extra resources, talents, even personal necessities, at the disposal of the local and the world community, is a witness to the Christian doctrine of property.

Naturally, the material resources that American Catholic women called on were those of their entire families so it actually was a family witness. From the gospel we learn that we hold property, or any of our possessions, not as an absolute right, but in stewardship. St. Thomas Aquinas stressed this when he taught that it is of precept, not of counsel, to share with those in need whatever we possess over and above our own necessities of life. By putting such teachings into practice, many Christians have effectively substituted for primitive capitalism, whose end was the spiralling of wealth without reference to moral norms, an economic way of life compatible with Christianity.

By donating to the needy what we have in abundance, we are moving towards what one of the Fathers of the Second Vatican Council called "a new meeting with poverty." Dom Helder Camara, Bishop of a poor diocese in northeast Brazil, in a document which he called 'an exchange of ideas,' told his fellow bishops: "Before engaging in reforms of any great depth, the Church has always met again with poverty." To the misery-scourged people of his diocese, he defined what he meant by poverty. "Poverty may, and sometimes should be a gift freely accepted from or even willingly offered to the Father. Misery, on the other hand, is revolting or debasing. It wounds the image of God that each man *IS*. It violates the right and duty of each man to accomplish his own integral self-fulfillment."

Dom Helder, well acquainted with those cities of Latin America where people live and fester around vast garbage dumps, where they weave in and out of sewage-filled alleys to reach one of the crumbling shacks that is called "home," asked for a deeper awareness of the theology of poverty. One of the most important developments of Vatican II occurred when dozens of bishops rose to speak on behalf of their people in the poorest corners of the world.

"If the Church is poor, as she ought to be," stated an African Council Father, "then she should correctly define herself as such and instruct the faithful about poverty. True poverty is not a question of external appearance," continued the Archbishop of Conakry, Guinea, the Most Reverend Tchidimbo. "The Church should speak out on the solidarity of all men. This solidarity implies more than charity, for as St. Thomas teaches, superabundant goods belong by natural law to the poor for their sustenance."

Bishop Edward E. Swanstrom told the Council Fathers

that in his journeys to misery-scourged areas, he had seen the biblical story of Lazarus the poor man and Dives the rich man enacted over and over again. Pointing out that he saw Lazarus "most obviously in a leprous beggar in a cart on a Calcutta street," Bishop Swanstrom added that he had seen Lazarus in refugee camps of Europe and Asia, begging not for food but for a place to live and work.

The press of the whole world took cognizance of the Vatican Council debate on world poverty when a layman was chosen to introduce the section on poverty in the draft of "The Church in the Modern World." The layman was James J. Norris, Executive Assistant to Bishop Swanstrom, and he spoke in flawless Latin, describing the problem first in poignant, dramatic terms: "Poverty means that a mother looks at her newborn infant knowing that it will probably die before the year is out." He then proceeded to give heart-stopping statistics drawn from the underdeveloped countries on infant mortality, illiteracy, and the widespread incidence of disease, and urged Christian communities in the nations of the world to "bring their influence to bear to encourage governments to continue and expand their policies for providing capital and technical assistance."

Speaking from his long immersion in a global anti-poverty and pro-refugee program, Mr. Norris warned: "No other group is likely to have the staying power needed for this long, arduous and often disappointing work."

It was out of such deep commitment and concern for the needs of the poorest members of the human family that the outlines of a new arm of the Universal Church were first seen. This arm would bring hope and strength to those among mankind who were closest to despair and death, and would mobilize the conscience first of the Christian world and then of all people of good will. It was designed as a Secretariat for Justice and Development to operate from the heart of the Church.

Another suggestion Dom Helder Camara presented in his ringing "exchange with my brothers in the episcopate" was that "we should deepen the doctrinal significance of the scene of the Last Judgment." And from this thought we return to the works of mercy, for these are the very matter of the Last Judgment.

In the age of overkill, when nuclear weapons are being developed that threaten untold millions with instant cremation, Christians may not be able to prevail on their governments to impose the ban on nuclear weapons called for by Pope John XXIII in *Pacem in Terris*. Neither have they the power to direct their heavy tax payments into the works of mercy desperately needed by the family of man, rather than into the nuclear buildup that threatens man's very survival.

They can, however, exercise their personal sense of responsibility and intensify the good that is possible of them. This good englobes such works of peace as clothing the naked and feeding the hungry. They would thus be ready for that scene when the Son of Man will come in majesty and accept or reject those before him on the simple test, "I was hungry and you gave me to eat; I was thirsty and you gave me to drink; I was a stranger and you took me in; naked and you covered me; sick and you visited me; I was in prison and you came to me."

Catholic women have been happy to make these works of mercy part of their daily lives. They have helped not only the person in need they could see, but also the needy separated from them by oceans and continents. Whether a near neighbor or a far one, they knew that to meet another's need is to meet Christ himself.

Afterword

ANYONE who has read to the end of these chapters must be profoundly impressed by the variety and effectiveness of the "works of peace" which they describe. Private dedication, personal charity and self-commitment, working within the great voluntary framework of an organized Church, can bring about miracles of realistic love and compassion. The scope for further work and effort by the affiliates of the National Council of Catholic Women is almost unlimited.

Yet the very success of the deeds of mercy recounted in *The Works of Peace* points us onwards to a larger commitment. In our own domestic society, we do not confuse charity and justice. Charity inside the nation, as in the world at large, is concerned with the extra sacrifice, the voluntary dedication, the "uncovenanted mercies" of neighborly good will. But the full community of the nation is based on the wider concept of *justice,* the right of each human family to share in some measure in the wealth all help to create, the obligation of the more fortunate members of society to underpin, through a progressive system of income tax, both the services—of health, of protection—from which all benefit, and the help—in housing or education—which poorer families cannot fully afford.

This whole dimension of "the general welfare" is now recognized, throughout Western society, to be the indispensable economic and social basis of a fair and open society. Its existence does not check private charity and alms-giving, because individual predicaments are always too varied to be completely covered by general rules and general assistance. But equally, private charity is no substitute for the larger operations of public justice.

Do we have to take notice of this larger dimension in world society? This is a profound question of principle for it affects every judgment we make about our relations with other states. As citizens we have to determine the limits of citizenship. Are we simply neighbors up to the frontier and strangers beyond? Do obligations cease at the seashore? Is there any real sense in which the word "community" applies to men and women living under different political jurisdictions?

As Christians we, of course, know part of the answer and have known it for two thousand years. In God's eyes there is "neither Jew nor Greek, male nor female, bond nor free." All are one in God. Brotherhood is the necessary consequence of God's Fatherhood. The Samaritan did not enquire about the race or nationality of the man in the ditch. And the God who sends his mercies down like rain upon "the just and the unjust" does not establish arbitrary drought areas according to the color of the country on the map.

This we have always known. But now three new dimensions are added to our knowledge. The first is the physical shrinking of our planet—through scientific revolutions in communication and transportation—to the size of a neigh-

borhood. By the time Major White had picked out the coast
of Texas, he was well out over the Pacific. A few minutes
more and China was within sight. We are not yet all astro-
nauts but anybody in six hours can fly over an ocean it took
months to cross in the Mayflower. This physical shrinkage of
space is a continuing and dynamic fact. The next aircraft will
take an hour for the crossing, the next perhaps ten minutes.
And by that time the spaceships will be off on interplanetary
discovery and we shall see our own planet almost as though it
were itself a spaceship, carrying the human race through
infinity. And if the crew of a spaceship is not a community,
nothing is.

The second scientific revolution is the revolution in resources. This, too, we know—but do we quite realize the
scale? Some four percent of the labor force of America can
now feed all the people of America on diets of a variety and
richness that have made obesity a national problem and
books on slimming a lucrative trade. In addition, they can
feed most of the rest of mankind as well—at least for the time
being. Or, to give another set of indices, the American gross
national product—the sum of all the goods and services produced in the United States—equalled about $630,000 mil-
lions in 1964. To this has been added over the last twelve
months a further $30,000 millions. This sum is equal to *all*
the goods and services produced in the whole continent of
Africa. It is equal to half the gross national product of Latin
America. In other words, the United States as a community is
not only twenty times richer than Africa. It *adds* almost casu-
ally to its wealth in one year the equivalent of all the wealth
of the African people.

This vast and growing scale of resources brought about by
constant innovation in science and technology—the hybrid

corn, the pesticides, new fertilizers, new sources of energy, electronics, the chemical revolutions which produce completely new materials—this cornucopia of expanding and diversifying supply makes it possible for the industrial nations to spend $120,000 millions each year on arms and still grow richer. Or launch a space program costing $20,000 millions and find that the by-products in electronic, fuel and rocket research stimulate whole new industries and whole new sources of wealth. As U Thant, the Secretary General of the United Nations, has often reminded us, in these days of almost unbelievable wealth, it is not resources that limit our imagination but imagination that limits our resources.

The third revolution is the simplest of all. With these same resources we can destroy spaceship Earth and desolate the home of man. Over all our concerns hangs the risk of atomic destruction. This is perhaps the final, inescapable proof of neighborhood—the same disaster can destroy us all.

So the world is new in three ways. It has shrunk to a physical neighborhood. There is almost no limit—in any but the very short run—to the resources available for action in any field. But action in war will end the human experiment.

This is the new world to which the oldest doctrines of Christianity have to be applied. Men are neighbors. There is enough wealth to transform the neighborhood. There is enough energy to destroy it. What, as Christians, must we do about these revolutionary but inescapable facts?

We have to follow the only route we know—and that is to copy the areas of peace and cooperation we have already established. Now we must apply the principles to our world society. This is not the place to go into the details of our *political* needs—for international legal codes and policing systems, for methods of conciliation and arbitration, for the

building up of a few key institutions of world order. Here
we are concerned with the works of charity and justice, and
in this field the need is clear—to accept for our world society
the obligations of justice and fair dealing which we accept
within our states.

First of all, the fact of obligation has to be understood and
accepted by the rich nations. Virtually all the states with
incomes per head of population of more than $700 are to be
found around the North Atlantic or in lands of European
settlement. In other words, it is the "white" Christian nations
today who represent the bulk of the world's wealth—they
make up between sixteen and eighteen percent of the world's
population and control seventy percent of its production, investment and trade. Christians may not be aware of the fact
but they are now a small wealthy elite in a world of poverty,
a white island of affluence in an ocean of distress. In Asia, in
Africa, in Latin America, two thirds of mankind have incomes of less than $200—often much less—and their attempts
at growth are still checked by a rise in population of three
percent a year. The gap between the Western Christian
minority and everyone else is widening.

So perhaps the first need among Christians in the West is
to be thoroughly aware of their astonishing privilege—to eat
enough, to be well clothed, to be educated and comfortably
housed, to have variety and choice—in a world where the vast
majority—as these pages so vividly describe—are hungry and
sick, work endlessly and die young.

Once the scale of the privilege enjoyed by Western Christians is recognized, then conclusions for action can follow.
Our need is to establish, in our wider world community,
some of the policies and institutions which underpin justice
and hope inside the domestic community. Two such policies

are particularly vital. The first is the progressive income tax which enables men and women, as their wealth increases, to make a proportionate contribution to the well-being of the whole community. Oliver Wendell Holmes once said: "With my taxes, I buy civilization," and since so much public money goes into education and health and better urban environment, it is profoundly true that public revenue does enhance the *quality* of life of the whole community and, in the shape of education, has also enormously increased the skills which help to produce the wealth in the first place.

In our worldwide society, we only have the first sketch of such a system—in all the forms of economic assistance that go under the heading of foreign aid. It is only a sketch because there is still no yardstick to measure the performance of each rich nation. "One percent of gross national product" has been constantly referred to as a possible standard. But at present only France conforms to it, and the United States which at one time during the Marshall Plan was giving two percent of gross national product, now gives only about 0.6 percent because its wealth has bounded upwards and its aid has not followed suit.

What is needed is a firm undertaking, possibly in an international treaty, that nations with an annual per capita income of, say, more than $700 will pledge one percent of gross national product to economic assistance programs over the next decade. Such a step would give the first formal institutional form to world solidarity and obligation—and would also permit all agencies working in the field of economic aid to perform their work with much greater efficiency and with the kind of long-term strategies that sustained growth demands.

A second field of advance in domestic society has lain in

giving the mass of the people a larger direct share in the output of the economy—by higher wages, by pension funds, fringe benefits and a variety of methods of profit-sharing, by encouraging investment in growth stocks. Henry Ford was a pioneer here, for he was the first to realize that higher wages would allow his workers to buy his cars. But by one means or another over the last thirty years—first in America and now in Europe—the great mass of the people are the largest factor in sustaining the market economy through their higher demand and they have received these powers of effective demand because more of the wealth of the economy ends up in their pockets. To this day, in Latin America, rural stagnation and low wages in the cities prevent the growth of demand among the masses and so keep the whole economy stagnant.

But we have very few of these mechanisms in our *world* economy. Here, as in nineteenth-century Britain, the economy still tends to work for the much greater benefit of the rich. The prices paid for the primary products of the poor nations—for cocoa, for coffee, for peanuts and for tea—tend to fall. All the benefit of capital investment from abroad, both public and private, in Latin America in the fifties was wiped out by falling export prices. Manufactured prices go steadily upwards. Western tariff structures seem designed to prevent the poor countries from processing their products and exporting the more profitable manufactured goods. All the "middle man" profits—in shipping, in insurance, in the organization of markets or credits—go back to the West. Substitutes produced by the new sophisticated chemical industries threaten to push out the natural goods—rubber, sisal, cotton—produced in the poorer lands. And foreign firms, investing in the poor lands, frequently exclude any local participation so that all the profits and capital gains flow back to the richer groups.

All these facts, assembled at last year's U.N. Conference on Trade and Development, add up to a world economy biased heavily toward the interests of the rich minority—and discriminating against the mass of poorer states.

Here then is another whole field for vigorous action to restore the balance and build up greater justice and fairer shares. Higher prices for primary exports, revised tariffs to assist industrial development abroad, easier credit to finance world trade, more local participation both in middle man services and in industrial ventures—all these are policies which will help to bring the poor nations a rather larger share of the world wealth they help to produce. Ten years ago, their share of world trade was about twenty-eight percent. Today, it is below twenty-six percent. Meanwhile they have to send out about eight percent more exports each year to buy the old volume of imports. Their position is slipping still further in relation to the wealthy West. We, rich already, are engrossing a *larger* share of world wealth. They, chronically needy, are making literally no progress.

There are, of course, other issues which could be discussed in this context—the strengthening of international institutions to help the work and underline the factor of world solidarity, the particular problems of population control, the whole vast field of technical assistance—particularly in education. But these two policies—*a better share of the world market and the acceptance of economic aid as an institutional fact in world society*—will, of themselves, go far to lessen the growing disparities and introduce the stabilizing principle of human solidarity into our precarious world.

But these steps will not be taken unless citizens inside domestic society in the West make steadily and widely and loudly known their support for this approach. Congressmen believe "there are no votes in foreign aid." Senators hear more from the militant opponents than from the vast mass of Christian voters who, once they think about the issue, must see that deep moral principles are involved. And so to the "works of peace" which can be accomplished through personal charity and dedication, the Christian people of the West need to add a further dimension—the "works of peace" that flow from brotherhood and from citizenship in the great city of man.

We are not simply political members of our own national groups. We belong to the human family and have the obligation there to establish the principles and institutions of justice and development. It is only half the work to be content—internationally—with voluntary good works. The new dimension of diminished space and vastly increased resources is the dimension of world justice as a practical and daily necessity. It is there that Christian citizens must make themselves strenuously and responsibly felt, educating their congressmen, pressuring their governments, seeing, in season and out of season, that there *is* a vast active constituency in favor of the *public* works of peace. It is precisely in this area that Catholic women can play a deepened and more crucial role. Committed as they are to the world-wide program of voluntary works of peace, their words have weight when they speak up for foreign aid, for technical assistance, for fairer trade, for working institutions in the world economy.

These are positive goals of responsible citizenship. But they are much more. Let us not forget our third fact—potential atomic war. What societies are peaceful—the divided, hate-ridden, poverty-stricken societies? Or the ones where wealth is shared and justice reigns? Are our crises today in Western Europe or North America or Australia? Are they not rather in the Congo and Saigon, in Santo Domingo and Cuba—all dependent, all a prey to shifting markets and falling prices, all heavily illiterate, all poor? Can we hope for a peaceful world if, year by year, the gap between rich nations and poor widens further and a sort of international class war breaks out to pit miserable against wealthy, East against West, colored against white?

But more than that, by what *right* should we then hope for peace? There are no promises of well-being in our religion for those who "sit down to eat and rise up to play." Our wealth is a trust and a privilege. It is a possible instrument of redemption. But if we do no more than gather it away in our barns for our selfish use, shall we not find that God's judgment on the rich man, "Thou fool, this night I will require thy soul of thee," has been extended to the whole of our rich community? We are all under judgment today. We have the means to act. We have the wealth to deploy. We have the elbow room of vast resources. But if we lack the will to use them in the works of peace and justice, not all this wealth and power and capacity will save us. We shall hear the Divine anathema: "Depart, ye cursed. . . ." And we shall deserve it.

BARBARA WARD